Broken Wounded & Blood Washed

ALEXA JONES

Broken, Wounded & Blood Washed

Authored by Alexa Jones

5.5" x 8.5" (13.97 x 21.59 cm)
Black & White on White paper 188 pages

Copyright © 2016 Alexa Jones
Cover Design & Formatting by Alexa Jones.
www.brandprofitstudio.com

All rights reserved. Royal Enterprise Publications.

ISBN-13: 978-1-68073-069-2

ISBN-10: 1-68073-069-X

Whoever loves his life loses it, and whoever hates his life in this world will keep it for eternal life.

John 12:25 (ESV)

Acknowledgements

Lord Jesus, thank you for all the time you take with me. Thank you for your patience, your kindness, your gentleness and all the things you share with me. Nobody fills my heart the way you do. Praisley, you get the mother of the century award for dealing with my intensely strong personality. I was a grown woman at birth and there was no way you could've ever prepared for raising me. To my sweet, loving husband Roy Charles Jones, Jr., I love you so much! I love you. I love you. You are such an amazing man of God and I am so grateful He brought us together to further His kingdom. You bring so much light, peace and comfort into my life. Your ministry of love towards me brought me to the place I am today. Thank you for making me your wife.

Table of Contents

When I Was Wounded

When I Was Wounded

When I Was Blood Washed

Introduction

My initial desire for writing this book was to lead women away from the path that leads to a dead end. I didn't want it to be another long and drawn out motivational book with a heart-wrenching sob story. This is for the Christian woman, the non-Christian woman, the looked down upon, talked about, the abandoned, the bullied and the left for dead type of woman. This is for the woman who can't seem to catch a break in her love life and/or in her personal life. This is for the woman who struggles to reach her dreams and the woman who finds herself in a constant puddle of tears. Most importantly, this is for the woman who's been touched. And when I say touched, I don't mean touched with the God fearing love she deserves, but a woman who has been touched by perversion that just seems to keep on following her everywhere she goes. Why? The odds say that likely woman is on a pathway to hell. Not only is she living in hell from day to day, but her life's journey is slowly dragging her to hell's eternal depths. If you find yourself offended by the former statement, I offer you my sincerest apologizes. I'm offended as well. I'm offended because Satan continuously works this strategy in the lives of women everywhere. In no way do I want to condemn woman to this place, but instead, I want to help them. I want to help break women free from self-defeating thoughts, sabotaging habits and bring them to a place of complete wholeness through the revelations and exercises in this book.

Chapter 1

When You Get It All Wrong

Wedding Idolatry

I have lived (*and I mean L-I-V-E-D*) for the day I would be seen in my wedding dress. Like most girls, I dreamed day and night of having that beautiful white, gloriously flowing satin gown. To me, a wedding dress is symbolic of a woman attaining the highest point of beauty, honor, protection, provision, love, and most importantly, respect. I wholeheartedly believed that if a man had love in his heart and decided to marry me, I would feel whole inside for once and marriage would change the direction of my life. Well... I got the dress. I met a nice guy named Cameron, stayed with him for a few years, and one day, he popped the big question. Overly excited, I immediately told him "YES!" I didn't pay any attention to all of the red flags I'd seen in our relationship and I completely ignored all the alarms going off in my head. I guess you could say I was geeked. I was too excited that someone finally loved me enough to consider marrying me. At the time, we were both just 22 years old. We both grew up in broken homes and we had no idea what we were in for in terms of marriage. Cameron was no more in shape to be a husband than I was to be a wife. And neither of us had any idea as to what qualities we should be looking for when choosing a suitable mate.

Where's My Ring At?

When Cameron proposed to me in the summer of 2006, I'd broken up with him a few days prior. At the time, I was suffering from a severe back injury, I'd just moved back in with my parents and had nothing to sleep on. He had promised to help me buy a new bed so I could recover better. But instead of helping me, he spent several hundred dollars on a video game system. When I saw that his priorities were completely backwards, I realized that I needed someone more mature in my life. After us being together for 2 years, I called it quits and hoped I would find someone who could demonstrate that they were serious about loving me.

One day while I was at work, I got a call from Cameron. He told me that he was desperate to meet with me and I agreed to meet him for lunch. Once he arrived, we began to walk down 4th street in Santa Monica, California. After about 2 blocks, he stopped me, proceeded to get down on one knee and started singing a song he wrote completely off key. He told me he loved me and assured me that he was ready to be the man I needed in my life. With his hands in the air, swaying back and forth to his off key singing, I couldn't help but notice there wasn't a ring in his hand. I thought it was great that he'd done this huge, corny public display of love and so I told him "Yes!" But my "yes" was conditional upon his ability to provide me with a ring. Like any woman, I wanted proof to show my friends and family that someone actually loved me. Once the initial excitement wore off, my pride took over. I dragged him to the mall immediately after work to buy me an engagement ring. Once we arrived at Kay Jewelers, the sales woman helped him pick out a two piece, half carat marquee diamond bridal ring. It was so beautiful and I fell absolutely in love with it. I was so distracted by the way the diamond sparkled and the promise of a better future that I completely ignored a lot of the signs that Cameron just wasn't ready to be a husband. Even though we were engaged, I noticed that anytime I tried to set a wedding date with Cameron, he would find a way to sabotage our progress. I often thought "Am I missing something?" I had reasoned in my mind that we were friends more than anything. We had great sex together, and most importantly, we went to church together.

Of course, I knew that what I was doing was wrong. I wanted to stop so badly but I desperately felt like I couldn't. Each time we'd fall into fornication, I would feel incredibly guilty. The guilt was overwhelming. My lack of self-control led me into an endless cycle of sex, praying, crying and telling God

I would not do it anymore. Even after repenting, I'd find myself back in bed with him again. Like a lot of lukewarm believers, I deeply loved the Lord in my heart, but my actions didn't show it. Fear was in the place where my faith should have been. I feared a future without Cameron more than I had faith in the power of God to fix my life.

Although breaking up seemed like a good solution, it was never one that lasted very long. Cameron was so desperate to keep me in our relationship that whenever I would mention breaking up, he'd pray with me, repent with me and agree to not having sex anymore. However, the very next day, he'd seduce me and I'd be drawn right back into the seemingly endless cycle of sexual sin. It felt like we were trapped and couldn't stop, not even to save our own souls. In all truth, we were more like rabbits than Christians.

Cameron had never seen an example of a holy, righteous, honest man of God in his life. Having sex with me was the only way he could demonstrate love. Although we were best friends, talked all the time, spent every day together and shared tons of laughs, I knew deep down in my heart that he wasn't the right man for me. Nevertheless, we were so close that ending our relationship seemed impossible. I really wanted a man of God. I wanted a man who knew how to touch me without touching me. I wanted a man who knew how to penetrate my being through prayer and not through sin.

As time went on and I saw he didn't reflect the qualities I really needed in a husband, I'd try and distance myself. Cameron never took this well. He hated rejection. He would be furious sometimes, while at other times, he would cry excessively. He would eventually resort to threatening my life in attempts to control me. Other times, he would call my cell phone repeatedly, leave endless amounts of text messages, or worst, he would come to my parents' home and scream my name from outside to humiliate me. Every effort he could make was made to make me feel extremely guilty for wanting to be free of him. He also made sure to place in my mind that if I ever left him, he would make sure that I had no future. I was his and he would be damned if another man had me. Even though things were dangerous for me, I didn't leave. I felt like nobody would help me. And besides, if anybody truly loved me, I wouldn't be in the situation I was in. From the looks of it, marrying Cameron was my only hope for a future.

My relationship track record prior to meeting Cameron told me that nobody thought I was worth committing to long term. Neither my father nor my step father showed any interest in covering me with the love and protection I desperately needed to feel from a male figure. And unfortunately, the men in my family weren't any better. I guess they figured that providing for and protecting their own daughters was enough for them. I was empty inside, so I allowed Cameron to withdraw from me over and over again.

The longer we were together, the more depressed I became. Deep down, I knew I wasn't loved. The depression, the anxiety, the self-condemnation, the hopelessness and feeling used took all their toll on me. It was hard to be kind to Cameron because I didn't trust him. Nevertheless, I felt stuck with him. Eventually, he began to feel unappreciated for what he believed he was giving to our relationship. And yet I often felt that nothing he gave me was beneficial to my life. When we'd gotten to the three year mark of our relationship and a year and a half into our engagement, I'd finally started feeling as if I could trust him. I reasoned with myself that he had been with me for three years and his staying with me was proof enough that we could work out forever, but Cameron felt differently.

He Broke Me

Once I'd gotten comfortable with him, Cameron decided to show me just how he felt about me as a woman. A few days after our three year anniversary, he'd stopped calling me and answering my calls. I was unable to reach him for three days. I knew something was seriously wrong because we talked every day. When your soul is tied to someone you can feel betrayal in your gut. At sunset on the third day, I went looking for Cameron, and I found him standing outside of his best friend's house. I jumped out my car and started screaming frantically. He calmly stood in place, feeling nothing and doing an excellent job of making me look like a mad woman. I was crying uncontrollably, so his friends walked away, and he simply told me that he would see me later. Later on, when we saw each other again, he admitted to cheating. He told me he was with a stripper. He told me she was better than me, skinnier than me, had longer hair than me, a larger butt than me and she had a butterfly tattoo on her navel just like he wanted. "I know you were trying to get there, but I'm sorry! SHE HAD IT!" he'd proudly exclaimed. I was stunned and my heart was instantly broken. Tearfully, I asked him to leave right away. He'd been having sex with her every day and every night for the three days that wouldn't take my calls. I knew Cameron could be vicious, but I'd never thought he would ever cheat on me and betray me. The betrayal left me traumatized. I called my family and asked for help, advice and a place to get away so I could process what had just happened to my engagement, but they ignored my pleas for help. Even going to church didn't help. Before that point, I had never known a pain so great than the betrayal of someone I trusted. My soul was on fire and I didn't know how to cope.

Having no self-esteem, sense of self-worth or safety, I took him back, but not because I was deep in love with him. I took him back because he'd threatened me and told me that even though he had cheated, he wasn't going to let me go. The betrayal left me feeling like I was dating a complete stranger. I was confused and I really had no answers. Initially, he'd lied so much about the events that took place when he'd been with the stripper, that it took five months of me questioning him to bring out the entire truth. Sometimes, I would just be going about my day to day business when, all of a sudden, I would put a few details together from Cameron's account of the affair and end up having to ask him more questions. I didn't know it then, but the Holy Spirit was exposing the depths of Cameron's deception and just how much he would lie to have his way.

At that time, I didn't have my engagement ring anymore. Nevertheless, I received several apology gifts for what he had done to me. He gave me a diamond heart necklace, a sapphire ring with matching sapphire earrings and a necklace that he purchased on credit. Our relationship was no longer secure. I didn't believe a word he said anymore, so I gave him an ultimatum. I told him to prove he really loved me by setting a date for us to have a wedding or I would walk away forever. Not wanting break up with me, He agreed.

An Aisle of Lies

Several months later as our wedding date approached, I placed a down payment on my wedding dress. But a few weeks later, I ended up having to return my wedding dress because Cameron had decided that he didn't want to get married anymore. He had only set a wedding date to buy himself more time with me. He didn't have the courage to voice that he didn't want to be married to me because he knew I would go and find someone worthy of my love. So silently, he had sabotaged the wedding week after week by not contributing to it. A few months had passed, and once I realized that there was no way we'd make our wedding budget, I took a deep breath and canceled the order on my dress. I canceled the venue. Mentioning nothing to family and friends, I found myself very ashamed that the man I'd spent the last three and a half years with and forgave after he'd maliciously cheated on me with a stripper, decided that I wasn't worth honoring with marriage vows. To him, I wasn't worth saving from embarrassment or humiliation at all. To him, I was garbage. I wasn't worth a single penny... not even a penny placed towards our future together. What I had were place holder words and a few place holder pieces of jewelry. I have to tell you, I'd looked at that jewelry every day and I never felt loved. I only felt hurt. None of the jewelry he'd given me was a sign of devout loyalty. They were apology gifts for him previously lying and cheating on me. Of course, I took the gifts because no one had ever given me jewelry before. What I wanted more than anything, was for my Cameron to heal me from all the wounds I'd gotten in our relationship.

In my mind, I had always believed that if a man really loved a woman, he would not wait any more than two years to marry her. At this point, my relationship with Cameron was coming up on its fourth year, and I had nothing to show for it other than a trail of tears. I didn't understand why he'd make me wait for what seemed like forever to marry me, and take me through all the pain he'd taken me through. I seriously doubted that he was ever going to marry me if I waited any longer than I'd already waited. From the very beginning of our relationship, I had a paralyzing fear that he would date me for a decade and never marry me. Or that he would use me for a long period of time until he thought he

had found someone better than me. I just didn't trust him.
How could I? Our entire relationship was built on one
fabricated lie after another. I didn't stay in the relationship
because I wanted to be in that relationship; I stayed because
I was afraid to leave. He was quiet, lying, possessive and
extremely controlling. Our relationship was rather sick, but
eventually, I married him anyway. It's not that he up and
decided one morning that I was worth it to him to make an
honest woman out of me. I gave him a choice to make. He
either had to marry me or I'd walk away. This time, he
simply felt too guilty to try and keep me anymore without
marrying me. That man had practically ruined me.

Married In Spite

In August of 2009, we married at our local County
Recorder's office, and I don't even think he ironed his
clothes for our wedding. It wasn't the happiest day of his life.
He felt trapped, unprepared, full of regret, and he had no
desire whatsoever to play the role of husband to a woman he

simply didn't value. I was nothing more than a possession to him.

As for my white dress... I decided to start my life as a married woman without it. I had done everything I could to get married and I'd given myself away at the cheapest price I could. I figured that somebody loving me was better than nobody loving me. Little did I know, the situation I had sold myself into wasn't one of love. If I'd known what love looked like, I would've known better.

He Hit Me

For the entire four years we were married, I found myself crying out to God every single day to help me escape that marriage. Despite Cameron's promise that he would never cheat on me again, he'd broken that promise and four months into our marriage, he had a mistress. When I tried to confront him about his affair, he physically attacked me, and the attack left me with visible injuries. He'd never hit me before we'd gotten married and I didn't believe he ever would. Over the course of our marriage, I couldn't seem to find myself. I only seemed to get more and more lost. Cameron would constantly leave me alone at our apartment, and he would only come home to have sex with me. Other than that, he made it clear that I wasn't worth spending time with and that he had other places to be and better things to do. I'd become pregnant by Cameron three times, and because of the distress I always found myself in, I miscarried every single child I'd conceived with him. Nothing on this earth can compare to the pain of losing my first child: my daughter. She was the light, love and absolute joy of my life.

After my first miscarriage, I worked hard to try and keep things going for myself. At that point, the economy was bad and I was unable to find work. I had no money at times, but I worked from home, freelancing web and graphic design. I even imported human hair extensions and sold them over the internet just to stay afloat. As much as I wanted to escape my marriage to Cameron, there was always a large part of me that wanted to stay. It wasn't because I loved him so much. He was horrible to me. I wanted to stay because I loved the marriage vow I made to God. I worked hard to keep us together but nothing I did to make the marriage better worked. Despite my efforts and constant communication, I was never good enough for him to cover me, protect me and provide for me. Talking to Cameron was like talking to a wall. He simply didn't care about my heart. I always dreamt that being a wife would be this big, beautiful, blessed, lifelong event of love and happiness. But as a wife, I felt lower than dirt. There were many days that I was suicidal. I would've rather been dead than to be his wife. As a matter of fact, as his wife, I felt as if I were already dead. If I left or tried to leave, he was going to kill me anyway. He made sure I knew that every time he choked me, held me down, threw me or tried to crash our car while driving. I was already dead, and nobody knew it but me. I tried getting help. I called domestic abuse hotlines, but no one answered. I emailed domestic abuse centers but never received a response. I was afraid to go to a shelter. I knew I'd be uncomfortable and eventually I'd come back home. Several times, I'd called the police, asked my friends for help, asked my church for help, and asked family for help, but at the end of the day, I had absolutely nowhere to turn.

I Lost It

One evening in December of 2012, I realized I couldn't take another ounce of deception from him, I locked myself in an office down the street from our studio apartment for an entire night to avoid going home. I knew that if Cameron lied to me anymore about us having a real future together, I would likely end up stabbing him repeatedly and I wouldn't stop. Hurting him seemed to be my only way out. I knew that if I left, he would hunt me down as he'd always done. But I also knew it could take a turn for the worse. Cameron was stronger than me and I knew that if I'd lashed out at him physically, he would have murdered me without remorse.

Once the sun rose and he left for work, I went to our studio apartment, packed my belongings, and I left in order to protect the both of us. I could not contain the rage I felt from all the lies I'd been told, the neglect, the humiliation, the fear, the trauma and the abuse. Finally, I was ready to unleash everything that man had given me and had very little concern about the consequences. If it were not for the still small voice of the Lord in the midst of my emotional inferno, there is no telling where we would be today. The Lord told me to call my counselor at the pregnancy clinic I'd gotten my ultrasounds at. My counselors name was Denise and she ended up being a voice of reason. She carefully and lovingly told me that it was best if I waited until I wasn't angry anymore before I returned home to talk.

During the few days that I was away from home, I found myself with nothing else to do but reflect on my marriage to Cameron. The more I reflected, the angrier I got because I had no cherished memories of us. I had holes in my shoes, no furniture in my apartment, one pair of jeans and I wasn't loved. I was mourning the loss of my babies all by myself, and it seemed nobody cared that I was a mother with no children to hold in her arms. Cameron never made any of it easy. He kept all his money for himself, hid it and selfishly spent our lively hood on his own selfish desires. At one point, we had even been four months behind on our rent because he felt that not having a roof over my head was not his problem. He thought I should give my entire income to the rent but never told me. On payday, he'd tell me he had bills to pay and just maybe, he would be able to give me some money towards the rent the following pay date. I simply had no more tears to cry. For 3 years, he lied every payday. Leaving me, his wife, completely stranded with the bills. My dress, my ring, my wedding, my children, my home, my honor, my vows... I'd given everything I had and had gotten absolutely nothing in return. I often wondered where God was in all of this. It took me a long time to realize, He simply wasn't in it. My husband wasn't in agreement to be my husband, and God was not going to move against Cameron's will. In this world, nobody has to love you if they don't want to. I couldn't fathom how I could have worked for so many years to establish a family, but ended up being dumped in the long run. Was God punishing me? Did God love me? Did I matter to Him? Did my desire to be a married woman matter to Him?

My idea or my idol of holy matrimony had been washed down the drain. Everything I felt that could have been finally pure and beautiful about me was now washed down the drain. Spiritually, I felt disgusting, spotted, blood stained... I didn't look like what I believed a woman of God should look like at all. I wasn't virtuous. I was hellish. Where on Earth did I go wrong?

I Was Guilty

I knew the answer to that question. I'd known it for a long time. I'd just hoped that even though I was walking in disobedience from God, that being married would save me from the consequences of sin. Marriage was supposed to be my savior. Marriage was supposed to be the way that I would make it up to God for fornicating, lying to Him, abusing our relationship and making my husband my god. No matter how much I prayed, God never corrected my husband when he did me wrong. He only protected me by alerting me when I was being lied to or was about to be harmed. God never allowed anyone to intervene with our marriage problems or to help us keep our marriage together. He simply didn't approve. It was clear that my spouse wanted nothing to do with God. And he didn't want to hear His orders that would often come through me because I had a prophetic gift on me. At that time, God had to divorce us. Yes, God divorced us. In the state of California, divorce takes six months, but in the realm of heaven, it is done when God says it is done.

For all that I had been through, God had to free me because I was in risk of hell's fire. If I had died, or if Jesus had returned, being in such a marriage that produced nothing but satanic fruit could have cost me my salvation. I was full of anger, malice, bitterness, covetousness, lust, grief, idolatry... every dark thing imaginable, even though I was a "Christian" and apparently "I loved God". I had no garment of righteousness. I had no Holy Armor. My wick wasn't trimmed. My heart wasn't circumcised. I didn't reflect holiness at all. I was a victim of perversion, and I reflected someone we all know very well: Jezebel.

Chapter 2

Meet Jezebel

The Spirit of Jezebel

Crafty and cunning in all its ways, the spirit of Jezebel is extremely subtle and very seductive. It has a thirst for stealing the show, and it's heavily known for causing men & women alike to fall. Jezebel is such a negatively influential character in the Bible that its name is grafted into our secular culture. When you hear somebody described as a Jezebel, it's never positive. It's usually used to describe a woman who has used sexuality, sensuality, manipulation and charismatic witchcraft in order to set herself up as a high ranking leader over a particular person or place. Whether it be over a family, ministry or a business, the way of Jezebel is to get what she wants through her body. Not only is the spirit of Jezebel controlling, but it is incredibly manipulative. Jezebel is great at sucking you into its emotions. A woman carrying a Jezebel spirit will usually tell you stories of betrayal so that you will sympathize with her will and her way. The spirit of Jezebel can even be hidden in the life of a believer, regardless of how outwardly holy that believer appears to be. The Jezebel spirit will always invite or attract perversion like a magnet until the host has submitted everything they have to the authority of Jesus Christ.

Has anybody ever called you Jezebel, even after you've done your best to live for the Lord? If they did, were you insulted? Were you hurt? There is something you should know. No matter how broken we are deep within, God will not give us (those who belong to Him) a license to obtain an abundant life through means of sin. Check yourself for the following things and know for certain that God is more concerned about repairing your broken mindset than using idolatry to mend your heart.

Are you putting men before God?

Have you had sex outside of marriage within the past three months?

Have you had oral sex within the past three months?

Have you been involved in masturbation within the past three months?

Have you watched pornography within the past three months?

Have you visited a strip club?

Have you participated in foreplay or sexual fondling within the past three months?

Are you in currently in possession of sexual objects used for sexual gratification?

Have you used or are you currently using a stripper pole to work out?

Have you done occult exercises such as yoga?

Do you meditate, chant, or focus on aligning your chakras?

Do you wear revealing clothing out in public or to church?

Do you feel convicted when wearing cleavage revealing tops, short skirts or fitted pants into the sanctuary of the Lord?

Do you often dream or fantasize about being with a man, thinking of all the sexual things you want to do to him?

Do you talk to men about your sexual past, leaving dirty thoughts inside their minds about what it would be like to be with you?

Are you convinced that you can be regarded as sexy and holy?

Do you have a strong desire for marriage and children that supersede any other desire in your life? Including the desire to obey God and wait until He brings those things to past?

Are you nervous or do you get anxiety about waiting or trusting God for your love life?

Do you beat yourself up and pick yourself apart in your private alone time because you haven't found love yet?

Do you find yourself either desperately submissive or fearfully controlling towards men you have attracted in your life?

Do these questions sound explicit? Well...they are! And unfortunately, explicitness is still a current reality for many women who profess to be followers of our Holiest High Priest, Jesus Christ. But none of these things sound like the Holiest of Holies at all.

If your answer to any of these questions is yes and you have not fully repented (changed your mind to NEVER do it again), you may be walking in perversion and not the office God called you to in 1 Peter 2:9. 1 Peter 2:9 reads,

> *"But ye are a chosen generation, a royal priesthood,*
> *a holy nation, a peculiar people; that ye should*

shew forth the praises of him who hath called you

out of darkness into his marvelous light."

To walk in perversion while God is holding you to the standard of the priesthood will lead you into trouble that you do not want to bear. To make matters worse, not only do you pollute yourself, you pollute the men and women of God and the eyes of unbelievers as well. If you're living in an ungodly manner, God knows why you walk in such a way. The comfort of another human being is soothing. This is why Jesus Christ said in James 16:7,"Nevertheless I tell you the truth; it is expedient for you that I go away: for if I go not away, the Comforter will not come unto you; but if I depart, I will send him unto you." Of course, the Comforter is the Holy Spirit. Have you ever really known Him? Have you ever really been in a relationship with Him, or have you discarded him for what you can see, hear and feel? He's committed to being with you, but are you committed to being with Him?

Once there was a young man named Isaiah, who I was really interested in. I had just gotten a divorce and I really believed that God put him in my path for a reason. We went out together twice, and the entire time we were together, he read the bible to me, didn't touch me, didn't kiss me and he always prayed and worshiped with me. Isaiah wooed me with the Song of Solomon and Proverbs 31 scriptures. I thought he was really handsome; plus he sang, rapped, worked as a D.J. and danced so beautifully. I was sure I had found my dream man, and I tried to find ways to position myself to prove to him that I could be his helpmate. I cried repeatedly and just continued to thank God for him. I wanted him to be in my life very much. My heart and spirit were completely open to him because I thought that there was absolutely no way I could get hurt by him. I felt like I couldn't breathe when he was away. But in all truth, I was sick. I was still depressed about my failed marriage and the damage that had been done in that marriage. I was deeply bitter from having miscarried my daughter and the loss of other pregnancies. Plus my low sense of self-worth left me extremely suicidal.

One day, Isaiah left to go on a trip for two weeks; he was going to be ministering in the desert. I didn't hear a word from him the entire time he was gone and it hurt me. It was obvious that he wasn't thinking about me at all and I didn't know how to handle it. With Isaiah, I'd begun to dream again, open my heart and hope for what I believed would finally be a chance at a real future. At times, I thought I was going to lose my mind. I wanted to go out and sleep with any random man because I was wounded and had convinced myself that I deserved and desperately needed someone to touch me. My insecurities and anxiety made me feel similar to what a person with a drug, alcohol or food addiction might feel. Somehow, someway we sometimes feel that we are deserving of sin. After the two weeks were over, Isaiah came back to California and called me. He said to me, "Hey, while I was out in the desert, the Lord was talking to me about children." With sincere passion in his voice, he continued, "I just want to let you know, I think you are so beautiful. When I get back, I would like us to go on an official date and take things to the next level." When I got off the phone with him, I cried tears of joy. I couldn't believe that for once in my life, a man had thought that I was beautiful and worthy of his love. And he treated me with kindness and not disrespect. I was on cloud nine, and I couldn't wait for him to get back so I could introduce him to my family. The following night, I called to check on him, and with full enthusiasm, he said, "Hey! I'm so glad you called. Listen, you know how I said that God was talking to me about children? I thought He was talking to me about you, but I was wrong. I can't keep seeing you because I just started seeing someone else... today! See, God just moved on me and this girl and did this thing between us! Right now, you're supposed to be dating the Holy Spirit." Needless to say, as I was standing there listening to the man of my dreams take his sword and drive it through my gut. I had very little words. I just felt like I wanted to faint. My vision was blurred for a few seconds. My joy was instantly gone. I was shaken up, in shock, humiliated, and I ran home from my office without my house keys. In the dark of the night, I bawled in my back yard. "Once again, nobody wants me!" I sobbed to myself. And this time, it simply hurt too bad and too deeply to try and fill those voids with sin. To add insult to the injury, the man of my dreams was giving his deepest affections to another person and felt completely confident that I should be left alone with the Holy Spirit. My thoughts were, "I can't touch Him, hear Him, or dance with Him; I am so lonely." Within two weeks, Isaiah had asked the girl to marry him and emailed me and invitation to their wedding, even though I hadn't had time to heal. I was so numb that I didn't care about my life or my soul anymore. I didn't care if I went to hell because I was in my own version of hell. How could someone have so much disregard for my heart? I ended up in one messy situation after another, and eventually, I found myself in a deep depression for about nine months. There were times when I'd be in bed for days with severe chest pain.

Eventually, God spoke to me. "The evil you are allowing yourself to feel is shutting down your heart valves. If you are going to leave this place, it's going to be painful. If you want to stay here, you have to speak to your heart and tell it to beat again." You see, the Bible states in Proverbs 13:12 that hope deferred makes the heart sick. And like many of you, at that time, there was nothing I wanted more than to have someone love me. I wanted to be of use and value to someone. Of course, I also wanted to have the amazing joy of being a mother once again.

Even though I was at my weakest, God pushed me to be strong and He left the choice of life and death in my hands. God held me fully accountable for my heartbreak and my depression for several reasons.

1. When I cried out to God to save me from my marriage and my mistakes, He had to make a message from my mess so none of it would be in

vain. I was carrying a ministry in my spiritual womb that I aborted because, once again, I'd ignorantly put a man who wasn't meant for me before my primary duties as a woman of God.

Note: If God has impregnated you with a ministry, you have to protect it with everything you've got until it comes to fruition. It's vital to your destiny, and most importantly, it's vital to the success of the kingdom.

What God has given you to do for Him is more important than anything you will ever accomplish on this Earth. Your assignment is even more important than the role of wife and mother.

It is our duty as Christians to be primarily concerned about the advancement of the kingdom of God more so than having husbands. Please know that your man of God wants a genuine woman of God. Doing Kingdom work takes work. If you are not working for the Kingdom of God, how will your divine ordained mate recognize you when he sees you? You have a ministry to do. It's time to get to work.

2. The Holy Spirit had already told me no regarding him, but I let my heart get carried away anyway.

Note: We have to learn how to listen to the Lord and not second guess Him. I made the mistake of thinking that even though the Lord told me no about Isaiah, my continued attraction to him would eventually lead to a yes. Isaiah 41:10 encourages us, "Do not fear, for I am with you; Do not anxiously look about you, for I am your God. I will strengthen you, surely I will help you, surely I will uphold you with My righteous right hand."

3. I was already wounded and broken.

I would've taken that man away from his assignment in order to nurse my wounds. I had no health in my heart nor in my mind. Many times Isaiah had prayed for me, and because he'd prayed for me in a way my ex-husband had never done, I was getting closer to a place of wholeness. Some wounds require a whole lot more attention than others to make sure they don't become infected.

Taking him away from his assignment would have brought him into a world of distress and introduced him to some of the demons I carried on a day to day basis. No matter how much he prayed for me, it was his love that I was allowing to make me whole and not the love of God. God is a jealous God. He doesn't want just anybody to have us. And He certainly doesn't want us putting anyone before Him.

4. I was too willing to be used by someone for the sake of having that person in my life.

I had to learn that people will use you and keep using you if you let them. When they are done (if they are ever done), they will discard you. Because I had failed at everything (being a student, a wife, a mother, a business owner, and more importantly, I was failing as a Christian every day),

I was trying to bring someone else into my life to make me feel worthwhile, instead of letting Jesus do it.

In no way, form, or fashion was I a suitable helper for a man of God. God had not gotten done making me into the woman He designed me to be. Every time, I jumped off the Potter's wheel before He would be done molding me, I would find myself incredibly broken and damaged again. And you know what? God would have to pick up all my fragments, soften me and work on me all over again.

5. He didn't choose me to be his bride, but I chose to be his wife.

Note: I was out of order! It is the proper order of the Lord that a man chooses a woman. Even though I thought I had great skills to bring to his ministry, Jesus told me that he hadn't asked for me. I was trying to give myself away to a man who hadn't even gone to my Father to get me. My self-esteem and self-worth were so low that I was willing to give myself away instantly and freely. Before he'd even asked for my hand in marriage, I had already eagerly accepted his proposal in my heart.

Wait for a true man of God who finds you serving faithfully in the Lord. It's then that he will know you are truly anointed to be a wife, and he will be able to see that you are indeed a good thing. If a man finds you outside of the will of God, he will find you in a mess, and he won't be able to see you in the spirit as the one he should marry.

6. Somehow, I had made Isaiah an idol.

Even though God said no to my relationship with Isaiah, I pleaded, cried, and petitioned God for him. All my hope for a better life were in being 'rescued' by him, instead of being fully submitted in total partnership to Jesus Christ. When he married someone else, I didn't want my life anymore, and I intentionally did things that could have ultimately destroyed my soul.

I had absolutely no right to consider destroying the vessel of the Lord simply because I'd made decisions that allowed

His temple to be filled with something other than Himself. If you have considered suicide, think clearly about how much more of yourself you are giving to that man than you are giving to the Lord.

7. My initial idea of being left with the Holy Spirit was the same as being completely alone.

I was insulted and grieved beyond measure when he told me I should be "dating the Holy Spirit". God needed to bring me beyond this broken thought process. In truth, it was an insult. But I'm sure the Holy Spirit was even more insulted that I was grieved and distraught about the idea of being intimate with Him. I treated the notion as if I'd been assigned a miserable prison sentence. Of course, my grief was largely due to my ignorance of who He really is.

Many times we miss the outpouring of God's love because we won't pay attention to the Holy Spirit. We miss the power of the Holy Spirit because we downplay Him as if

He is just as unreal or unimportant as Casper, the Friendly Ghost. Little do we know, the Holy Spirit is the most valuable ally we have in this whole entire world. Nobody will be there for us the way the Holy Spirit will be there for us. My relationship with Him has grown so much that I now value the time I get to spend talking, listening, and waiting for Him.

8. God was done babying me. We'd been through this before.

If God had nursed my pain, He would have been feeding into my perverse mindset, and this would have done more harm to me than good. When worldly men nurse our pain, they do it and pervert us even more. God won't send that kind of help. He wants us healed through our dedication to living lifestyles of purity and holiness, just as He'd lined out in His Word. When we are in a position of holiness, we are in the right position to receive the full stream of Apostolic power that He has for us. This takes maturity and great effort on our part.

Learning to Be Whole

More than I longed for a warm body, I longed for spiritual oneness. But God deeply desired for me to have that oneness with Him alone before He would present me to anyone. If I'm not one with Him, He cannot truly know me in an intimate way. The Bible states in Matthew 7:23, "And then will I profess unto them, I never knew you: depart from me, ye that work iniquity." Knowing Him and having an intimate relationship with Him is something we must press towards while we are single and continue in when we are married. When God is looking for beauty in you, He's looking for your holiness. There is nothing about your outward appearance that is enough to make you acceptable to Jesus Christ. There is nothing in this world that makes you more beautiful to God than the holiness you carry within you. And I don't mean your holiness during your religious acts on Sunday morning, Tuesday night and Wednesday afternoon church services. What I mean is the holiness required for God to be able to use you in mighty ways. The type of holiness that produces great works in the Spirit and edifies people's lives. I'm talking about holiness that heals the bodies and restores the minds of those who are broken.

All the Single Ladies

Some time ago, God gave me a dream that was very relevant to our culture today. He showed me a hotel room in a high rise building that was dark inside. There were two elevators in the room on separate corners. The elevator on the left was dark and quiet. The elevator on the right was full of light. There was a girl in the hotel room who was getting dressed for the night. She was wearing a very revealing sequined blue mini dress, five inch blue stiletto heels and red lipstick. Apparently, she loved a very popular pop singer that dressed the same way. This girl had listened to this pop singers music day in and day out to the point where the singer's ways were now her ways of living. She deeply believed that she needed to be overly sexual, attention seeking, sexually promiscuous, cutthroat and trashy in order to make it to the top in life.

As the girl prepared to leave, she grabbed the hem of her dress and tugged on it to pull it down over her derriere because the dress didn't cover her well. She looked at both elevators. She pondered if she should take the quiet, dark elevator on the left or the well-lit elevator on the right. Not only was the elevator on the right well lit, the singers music was playing loudly on the inside of it. Of course, being ready to party, the girl entered the noisy elevator. When she entered the elevator, the doors closed. When she pressed the button to take her to her desired destination, the elevator would begin to shake violently. The elevator shook so violently that it opened its doors and threw her out on her butt. The problem? Such a path of life was completely unfit for a daughter of God. Such a path would never work for her. It would only bring her to humiliation, shame, and ruin.

She pondered what she'd just gone through, and when she looked into the quiet, dark elevator, she saw God in the elevator. She didn't want to enter the elevator that God was in. She was determined to get a quick fix to everything she needed in life, regardless of what it took. She tried fervently to get back into the well-lit elevator that was blasting the singer's message to women. She wanted it to take her to her desired destination. Lo and behold... the elevator kept spitting her out each time she entered it. Finally, it stopped allowing her to enter it. She was sealed with the blood of Jesus. She had been bought with a price!

She climbed to the top of the elevator to see if she could get in through the ceiling since she couldn't get in through the doors. She was willing to take drastic measures to avoid going God's way because:

- It's not well lit. The pop singers elevator was illuminated with show lights.

- It was quiet. It didn't play the music she wanted.

- It was lonely, yet more intimate than what she was ready for. God wanted to make her whole, but she wasn't ready to receive it.

- She was inappropriately dressed. She wasn't dressed for God, so she was ashamed to go in His presence.

- She was afraid. She desired a man who would love her. The singer however, demonstrated that it could be done right before her eyes if only she followed her example. God was requiring the girl's faith only.

The moral of the story is that God has a better way for His daughters, but many are afraid to take it. Many refuse to believe that God can provide them with husbands after His own heart. Many don't believe that they can ever be loved by a man if they don't first give up their bodies. Neither Jezebel nor any of today's secular music artist (who follows after Jezebel's likeness), will ever lead women to good, Godly men. We should never decide to obey God for the sake of getting husbands; we should be obedient to God because we love Him and desire to be in His will for our lives. His desire is that we'd be holy inside and out, and the only way we walk in the beauty of holiness is by walking alone with the Lord and leaving the way of the world behind. For many are called, but few are chosen. For those who are chosen, nothing will work out for you until you decide to leave the deceptive pathway of wickedness and walk in the truth of who God called you to be.

For what good does it profit a woman of God to gain the whole world and lose her soul? Especially a soul that she has given to Jesus Christ. You've heard it before, and I will say it again: You are not your own. You have been bought with a price. Jesus didn't died for you just to give you an excuse to keep living a life of sin. Every day, He waits for you to leave the seductive clothing behind. He waits for you to leave the seductive mindset behind. He waits for you to quit flirting and enticing men to think about you sexually. He waits for you to come out of the club, stop dancing seductively, smoking, and drinking. He wants you to sit still before Him so He can wash you clean with the water of His Word.

The Lord has been trying to prepare you for Himself because He is only coming back to rapture a spotless and wrinkle free bride. This means He has got to clean you up and iron you out so that what He has called you to be, will be fulfilled.

God knows that you hurt. God knows you are afraid. God knows some days you don't feel vibrant and you just need anything you can find to make you feel alive again. He even knows you are lonely and sometimes halfway out your mind, but the Spirit of the Lord is saying to you, "Leave these things behind My love. Consecrate yourself to Me. Allow Me to purify you. Allow Me to give you a virgin's heart again. Let Me dry your tears so that no man can prey on you. Let Me fill up the holes in you so men won't stick their hooks so easily into you, draw you near to themselves, only to throw you back out into the sea. Allow Me to show you your worth.

Repent and change your mind about the pathways of wickedness while it is still yet today. Eternity is a long time My love, and I desire that you spend it with Me. **A warning to you: If you continue to lie down in the beds of men who are not your husband, lie with strange women, seduce groups of people through lewd dancing, drink strange drinks, and fill your mind with demonic music, I will have to fulfill my word in Revelations 2:21-23.**"

Revelations 2:21-23: And I gave her space to repent of her fornication and she repented not. Behold, I will cast her into a bed, and them that commit adultery with her into great tribulation, except they repent of their deeds. And I will kill her children with death; and all the churches shall know that I am He which searches the reigns and the hearts: and I will give unto every one of you according to your works.

The Space to Repent

God giving you the space to repent is the greatest thing that will ever happen to you. You've said over and over again, "God knows my heart! God knows I just want to be loved! That's why I do what I do. There is no other way."

Yes, God knows your heart. **And if you've said these things in your heart, the Word of God is true when it says that the heart is "deceitfully wicked."** You've listened to the whisper and sometimes loud blaring suggestions of the serpent for so long that you have believed and listened to his doctrine. The only problem is that the gospel of Satan is a lie. It never leads to anything good for anyone, whether they are a child of God or not. God knows you are bombarded with Satan's lies and suggestions. He knows the lies that are recorded in your mind. He knows that the lies are before your eyes through your culture. What God wants to know is, when will you stop listening to your heart and start listening to Him? You have to power to silence the world anytime you desire to hear the Word.

When will you stop glamorizing sin? God left you His Word so that you can increase your faith. Remember, faith is the substance of all the things you hope for. Your belief in the things of God is a real and living thing.

God, in His goodness, steps away so that you can live your life. He knows you are hurting deep inside, leading you to make the decisions that you make. So God waits and gives you space to repent, but He won't wait forever. There will come a day when the door of grace will slam shut, and it will be too late for anyone who's not on the other side of it. If that someone is you, on that day, you won't have any more excuses because God had given you plenty of time to repent.

Hidden Idols

One of the greatest things God will do for you is fulfill His Word in your life regardless of what your life looks like. God has something special just for you.

The first commandment God gave Moses was this:

"Thou shall Love thy Lord thy God. Thou shall have no other Gods before Him."

You see, all the balance of your entire existence hangs on this first commandment. *Every single thing that we put before God will ultimately fail us.* This command is for our own good, and the strength of our own lives. It's not God who needs us to love Him. It's us who needs to love Him.

The second commandment God gave Moses was:

"Thou shalt make no graven images to bow down and worship them. I am the Lord thy God. And I am a jealous God."

Maybe you are not quite aware of it, but carving and idol of wood, glass or stone isn't the only way to make a graven image. We can create a graven image in our minds. When we carve out something in our minds, and that thing takes precedence over God, we have made an idol to bow down and worship. It can be a fantasy that you have or, something you are willing to deliberately disobey God in order to obtain. For example, some people make idols out of marriage. For me, the graven images I had in my heart were:

The idea of having a perfect family because I came from a broken home.

Having a wedding, and finally being honored by friends and family for something I'd done well.

Being the youngest black fashion designer to present a collection at New York fashion week. Having to drop out of fashion design school made this impossible.

The graven images can even be bad memories such as memories of neglect or abuse. It's not that we are in sin because something bad happened to us, but we are in sin when we hold up those memories against the will or Word of God with the intent to disobey Him.

If Jesus were to stand in front of you and ask you, "Why haven't you come to me? Why haven't you obeyed me?" What would you tell Him?

There was a time when I would have had a long list of answers for Jesus if He'd ever asked me that question. Those answers included:

I've been depressed.

I'm really overwhelmed.

I'm suffering badly from anxiety.

I'm suffering from post-traumatic stress syndrome.

I'm lonely. Really, really lonely.

My father never wanted me and it still hurts.

My mother never poured anything good into me.

My family never helped me; they just left me hanging by the wayside.

No man has ever loved me. Everyone just uses me.

My husband abused me and never covered me.

I miscarried three children. I'm a grieving mother with unspeakable pain.

I lost my home, and now, I'm homeless.

I have enough excuses to write a book with. I've cried enough tears over my life to probably fill a small pond, and each one of those excuses represented a piece of me. They were graven images in my mind and spiritually broken pieces of my heart that I kept in a special place all to myself. I kept fragments of my graven idols deep within my heart. I grew bitter and I refused to completely give any of those broken pieces over to Christ. I refused to let Him heal me, and I held up each one of my idolatrous excuses to His face.

I was so wounded by life that I couldn't fully forgive the people who'd hurt me. Someone had to pay, even if that someone was me.

Jesus had given me given His entire body, shed all His blood and sacrificed His life on this Earth for me, but I couldn't seem to walk away from my broken heart. I worshiped it daily because each event that had shattered my heart was on my mind constantly. I allowed those graven images and emotions to be the leaders of my life more so than God. Of course, in my heart, I loved God very much. But when I had to make some of my deepest decisions, I'd turned to my pain to lead the way.

It wasn't until I began to see what I was doing that I began to bow down on my face in prayer and tearfully give Jesus my deeply hidden idols (my excuses) one by one. I told Him that I didn't want anything to come in between my relationship with Him anymore, not even the bitterness from losing my children in the abusive marriage I'd survived.

God wasn't going to give into my Jezebel-like ways. He wasn't going to be moved by the manipulation of my tears. I had manipulated myself enough. He simply stood back, and with unconditional love in his words, He said, "When you are ready to own up to the consequences of the sin you have brought upon yourself, then I will be here waiting to heal you." I sinned. Point blank. Period. I paid the price for the sins I had committed in my past. I'm sure God saved me from even worse consequences. I couldn't wrap my mind around why it seemed like others were "getting away" with going the same path I had gone down, but I couldn't seem to get away with my sins I suffered because of them. At one point, I'd lost everything I loved and ended up with nothing. I was angry and humiliated. Nevertheless, I had to find a way to have a better relationship with God, even though I was incredibly bitter and hated my very existence.

Yes, I'd worship the Lord. Yes, I'd pray to the Lord. Yes, I stopped having sex. But to sit alone and talk with a God I only heard in my dreams and couldn't physically touch seemed absurd, even though I could sometimes feel His presence. It was then that I knew I had to get to a place in my mind, heart, and soul where I'd stop allowing the darkness of my past to keep me from the redemptive power of Jesus Christ.

Most importantly, what I want you to learn from my testimony is that God has a better way for you than the way of sin as outlined by the world. Gone are the days when we could afford to tell God "no" or "wait". We have so many warnings, information and tools at our disposal that when we stand before Him on the Day of Judgment, we will be without excuse.

If you are ready to make the change required to walk into the greatness that God called you, then please pray the following prayer out loud over yourself:

Heavenly Father, I come to You in the name of Jesus to repent for my sins, my lifestyle and any wrongful mindset I have that goes against the biblical standard You have given me. I'm ready to repent of my sins and begin my journey to being perfect and powerful in You. Lord, I renounce every idol and graven image in my past or presence that I have held up as an excuse to You. I renounce every soul tie I have created with the people I have joined myself to through sex. I renounce soul ties created with people in my life that have hurt me, abused me, rejected me, used me and abandoned me. Lord, I desire with my whole heart to be free today in Jesus name. Father, I pray that You guide me on this journey of deliverance and that You make me ready, pure and spotless for the day of your coming above all things. In Jesus name, I ask these things, Amen.

Intimate Prayer Exercises to Bring You Closer to God

Repent for every person you've been sexual with by name. Ask God to restore wholeness to you and the previous partner.

Renounce the soul ties you established with that person by name. Thank God that it is broken by the blood of Jesus.

Forgive every person who has misused or abused you by name.

Repent for using any sexual toys, sexual stories, or pornography to seduce yourself or your lovers. Decree that any open satanic doors or satanic portals in your life be closed in Jesus name.

Repent (by name) for idols (whether dreams, people, entertainment or memories) that you've place before God.

Ask God to restore the years the enemy took from you, and those you foolishly gave away.

Things That Should Be Different In Your Life

If you are ready for a true transformation, it starts within the heart. One of the first things you want to do is get rid of the sinful memorabilia of your past life before you dedicate your life to Christ. It's very important that you tear down your altars. This includes, but is not limited to:

Music – This is VERY important. I had an entire season where God had spoken very heavily against Beyoncé and her music to me. It was a heavily influential doctrine used by Satan to deceive the masses. If you have ungodly CD's break them in pieces. If you have MP3's... DELETE them!

Apparel – God invented fashion, but His vision for fashion is that it should be modest. I'm not saying your skirt should be down to your ankles, but I am saying that it should not reveal your thighs or derriere. Here's a rule of thumb. If you wouldn't wear it standing in the presence of Jesus Christ, it needs to go.

Lingerie – Any lingerie used in acts of fornication needs to be destroyed. This includes lingerie that was given to you as gifts. Why? Your lingerie could very well re-attract the same spirits that you recently cut ties with.

Love Letters – Words are powerful, especially written words. If you've written love letters and you no longer have them, renounce the words of those letters before God in prayer. Little did you know, you were contracting affections for the wrong person in the Spirit realm.

Friends – This is usually a tough one, but you are heavily influenced by your environment. Ask God to show you which friends should remain in your life and which ones should not.

Boyfriend – In reality, you don't want a boyfriend. You want a husband. A woman of God has no time for a boyfriend. She has a kingdom to build for the Lord. Ask God if the man in your life intends to marry you. If not, that man needs to go so that God can properly prepare you for the man He is sending to be your husband.

It is absolutely vital to our relationship with Jesus that we don't resemble the enemy in any way, shape form or fashion. There are many who live their lives paying God lip service, thanking Him for the sins they are able to commit. Woman of God, trust that you do not have to turn to the influence of the enemy to get anything that God says is for you. God alone knows the way to get to your blessing. Simply trust Him, obey Him and follow the way He is leading you to go.

Chapter 3

Meeting Jesus

Returning To Our First Love

I had been a Christian since the age of nine. I remember when I first chose to go down to the altar and accept Jesus as my Lord and Savior. I'd made this choice myself, and to be honest with you, I think I was too young to understand what I was doing. All I knew was that even at nine years old, I was empty and I really wanted to belong. I wanted to fit in somewhere, and at the time, it seemed like the church was just the place to do it.

To my surprise, I didn't fit in at church at all. I felt like the Sunday school teachers were nicer to the kids who were better looking and better groomed than me. I also felt very hurt by my inability to make friends with other Christian children. I wondered how I was supposed to experience the love of God if I couldn't get any of His people to love me. I found myself rejected and isolated in my youth, and even though I didn't have good experiences with people, I was still able to draw closer to God because the isolation I'd experienced developed a longing in me for Him. I talked to Him all the time before I even knew how to listen. I cried to Him all the time before I even knew how to stand strong. I knew of Jesus, but to tell you the truth, I didn't understand Him for a very long time because I didn't see Him demonstrated in the people I came into contact with. As I grew older, my heart waxed hard and waxed cold. I didn't believe that Jesus loved me, and I always felt like God was out to get me. It felt like He ignored every tear I ever shed over the trials I had experienced in my young life. Truth be told, the thing that kept me from experiencing the light of God was that I allowed my heart to be constantly covered in darkness.

But Jesus Had Hope for Me

God never promised us perfection. He did, however, state that we would experience trials and tribulations. Being bullied over my height, my hair, my gapped teeth, and my weight all the way up to my sophomore year in high school was truly devastating. Regardless of what people did to break me down, God still had plans for me. I used to wonder why kids would single me out and pick on me. Now I know that all those attacks were demonic and sent to break me because of the great anointing God had hidden in me. It was an anointing that I knew nothing about. I was a target for the promise I carried.

What I didn't know was that even though life tried to tear me down, God had reserved a day when I would be set apart so that He, Himself would esteem me. God doesn't want to share His Glory with anybody! What I also didn't know was that in my spiritual womb, God had planted a seed that would birth forth the next generation of strong and mighty believers. I don't currently have the children that I desire, but glory to God, I am certain that this book is reclaiming His daughters so that they can be born again in the spirit!

The enemy believed that he would make me a forever victim, but God had already spoken before the beginning of time that He would make me victorious, just like He will make you victorious. When people decided that I wasn't worth a decent compassionate touch, God said. "Daughter, you are just right for My touch!" When nobody would work to help heal my wounds or my broken heart, God stated in the love letter He wrote to me "the Bible", that He came just for me. He came to heal my broken heart and bandage my gaping wounds. When I lost hope for my life, God had already preordained in His Word that the thoughts He had about me were good and that He had given me hope for a certain future. When I was in a state of untreated mental illness because of all the afflictions to my soul, the Lord had already healed and restored me. He came before I was even born to make me whole, even before I'd been broken by the world.

JESUS CHRIST HAS ALREADY DONE IT FOR YOU. WHATEVER YOU NEED, ALL YOU HAVE TO DO IS RECEIVE IT!

Regardless of the many souls who have pulled away from you, the compassion of God will always lend its hand to you.

Understanding Who Jesus Is

Do you know and fully understand who Jesus Christ is? Jesus Christ wasn't just man that lived over two thousand years ago. Jesus is the Word of God, the very power He used to create you. Jesus existed in the beginning of the creation of mankind. Through the light of Christ, God made everything that existed on this planet, including you. We find evidence of this in John 1:1.

Where is this light of Christ?

The light of Christ is within your spirit, and the job of your spirit is to convert your soul to have an incredibly intimate relationship with your Maker before you leave this planet. When we die, all of our spirits will return to God, but our souls have a choice to make as to where they will spend all of eternity.

Why do you need an intimate relationship with your Maker?

You need an intimate relationship because your Maker has a calling on you that goes beyond your human comprehension. You have a calling to priesthood, holiness, royalty and uniqueness. It's a calling that is profound within the earth. Without this intimate relationship, several things can happen (if they haven't happened already), and they include:

1. We can become fully open for satanic seduction, suggestion and influence.

2. We can find ourselves repeatedly tainted and spotted by the darkness of sin.

3. We can become prime and easy targets for the enemy.

4. We can grow in deadly sins such as bitterness, anger, lust and greed.

5. Living virtuously can become an incredibly difficult fight day in and day out. Without intimacy with the Spirit of Christ, we will lose the majority of our battles.

6. When the storms of life come, we will find ourselves tossed to and fro, clinging to idols instead of what makes us whole.

7. We'll be lead down a very wide path that ultimately leads to destruction and eternal death.

Without this intimate relationship with our Maker, who is our Husband, we are in adultery, and a scarlet letter is written on us in the spirit realm for all to see and treat us as adulterers and adulteresses. Have you ever noticed how your own family or peers can treat you as if you're tainted? Have you noticed how some would-be lovers won't fully commit to a life with you, and you can never seem to reach the place you need to be in life? Often, when you don't understand why you suffer through the rejections, you begin to pick yourself apart. You begin to drop your price. You devalue yourself. You can't figure out your worth. I know I don't need to paint this picture for you. You know the depths of yourself and often wonder, why is it that you're not chosen, helped or loved by family, other Christians or the men you thought would one day be the saviors of your life. Because of this, many women have found themselves banging desperately on the doors of their fairy tales, doing any and everything they can to get inside their imaginary happily ever after's. Many women think that men hold the keys to their happiness, and they find themselves doing anything they can to win their Prince Charming.

Some women wonder why they have to be intimate with an invisible God they don't understand when they can be physically intimate with a real man. The truth is that no matter how intimate you are with a man, it's possible for you to lack understanding of who he really is. Why? Because wide is the way that leads to destruction (through many men) and narrow is the way that leads to everlasting life. That narrow way is through your personal devotion to Jesus Christ, whether you're on your knees or laid prostrate before Him. He alone is worthy of all the glory because He redeemed your soul from the depths of Hell.

How does Jesus redeem me when all I've seen is everyone leaving me? Jesus knew everything you would go through in this wicked, wicked world. He knew you would be molested. He knew you'd be raped. He knew you'd be abandoned physically and/or emotionally by one or both of your parents. He knew your first love would lie to you and leave you with a broken heart. He knew your heart would be broken over and over again. He knew you'd try to find value by giving your body to men who would use it for their own, selfish pleasure, and they'd leave you broken and abandoned. He knew all the people who would humiliate you. Jesus knew you would be angry, depressed, bitter, walking in rebellion, un-forgiveness, nakedness, and fear, with no relief in sight...not even in church. He knew Satan would touch you, and you'd be living with a mind of sin, death and deep regret.

Woman of God, Know This

Jesus has hope for you.

Jesus has beauty for you.

Jesus has promise for you.

But you have got to keep following Him with all you've got.

So What Happens Now?

What happens when you are alone with yourself and no one else? What hope do you have when you read or hear the Word of God and you just don't feel good enough? What happens when you don't make the cut for a spotless bride ready for the return of Christ? Or when you are emotionally bleeding, broken and wounded all over. What do you do when you are drenched in your tears and the stain of your former sins?

I say it's time for several things to happen. It's time to be baptized in the Spirit, washed with the Word, cleansed by the blood and transformed by the renewing of your mind. No matter what has plagued you in your life, Jesus is able to heal you from it all. No matter how many people have touched you in your life, you are never too defiled for the Lord. As a matter of fact, Jesus healed a man infested with thousands of demons. When he cried out to Him, Jesus delivered him from each and every single demon. Jesus even went to the horrible, repulsive depths of hell for three days when He died. There is absolutely nothing too deep or too dark for Him to deal with.

If you find yourself feeling this way, allow the power of God to remove the wounds from your soul and the marks from your Spirit. Do not allow your wounds to be your god anymore.

Discipleship

The power of Christ is not only living within us, it also has the power to heal us. Jesus is our great physician. Some time ago, God had shown me a vision of the modern-day medical industry. He showed me masonic occult activity within the industry. Sitting above a massive checkered floor were castles. As I looked up in the castles, I could see American doctors practicing witchcraft on their patients. They were making them even sicker than they were, rather than healing them. They were working on drugs to create more illnesses because the more people who were sick, the more money they would earn. When people are sick and dying, they become desperately willing to spend whatever amount of money they can to help prolong their lives here on earth.

This is why Jesus is referred to as, not just our physician, but our Great Physician. He alone has the power to heal and purify our minds, bodies, and souls. When we find ourselves desperate for love and restoration, it is vital that we turn our care over to Jesus Christ, instead of a man. Many times, wounded women believe they need to be nursed back to health, but Jesus desires to empower and build them up. He desires to care for and make provision for us, instead of nursing our pain. When a man sets aside time to nurse a grown woman, he is getting her in a position to pervert her because she's a weak and easy kill for the lusts of his heart. Many women mistake this babying for love, and when a woman falsely perceives these behaviors to be love (especially if she has never received the healthy nurturing that should have come from a father while growing up), a wounded woman will gladly pay up front for emotional care, believing that constant attention from the right man will make her better. Why does she think this? In truth, love has always cost her something. Sometimes, she paid with her body, mind, talent or her money... Love has *always* cost her something. Jesus's love doesn't cost us anything, but an eternity with Him will cost us everything. His deepest desire is for all to know Him intimately so that we are inspired and have the direction we need in order to do His will. You need to know that you are automatically worthy of God's love.

At the Feet of Jesus

Have you ever sat down or bowed down at the feet of Jesus when you were praying? Our tears are precious upon His feet. Our tears upon His feet are an honor to Him. It is a sign of our devotion, surrender, appreciation, and repentance.

You Are Qualified For Christ.

Jesus did not come for those who were well, but for those who are sick. Have you obtained a disease as a result of the choices you've made in your past? Jesus can cleanse you and make you whole, regardless of what you were diagnosed with. Whether it was herpes, HIV, AIDS or anything else, Jesus is able to cleanse you. Freedom, healing, and deliverance will require several actions on your part. Remember that you have the dominion and authority over unclean spirits. You must also know that Jesus loves you and is willing to make you well. When praying for your healing, keep these prayer points in mind:

Be truly repentant for the sins you committed.

Ask God to go back in time and repair the damaged parts of your life that have become the foundations of your choices.

Break generational curses. It's important to ask God to replace any broken foundations with the foundation of Jesus Christ. For example, if you have parents (and grandparents) who've affected your life with their bad habits and unloving ways, break those generational curses and declare that you are standing on the foundation of Christ.

Fast for a day, drinking water only, and ask the Lord to guide you to holiness. The Lord will begin to reveal to you the areas of your life that need to be sealed off so the enemy won't have access to you anymore.

Forgive, forgive, and forgive some more. Demonstrate that forgiveness by praying that your offender is blessed with God's best.

Submit your entire life to the will and the way of the Lord. You will need God's help if you are going to be successful in the new future.

Keep your faith. Never give up on your confession of healing. Never stop decreeing and declaring your healing, regardless of the doctor's report. Expect to see results and consistently remind the evil attacking your body that it is under your feet.

Divine Intimacy That Cant Compare

Absolute oneness between two people requires three things.

1. Agreement

2. Walking and operating together

3. An intimate relationship

You know, two people can act like a couple and not be a real couple if any of these three things are missing. In the event that you operate together, but you are not in agreement to be in a Holy marriage, it will cause a breakdown in the relationship. One might even feel used. Or let's say you are in agreement to be married, but there's no spiritual intimacy in your relationship. In such a situation, you will become heartbroken. One of you may feel incredibly defrauded and cheated on from participating in a relationship without intimacy. After all, we all need intimacy. If you are not intimate with the one you claim to be in agreement with, you are giving that person's time to someone else, and this simply isn't right. When we give the time we are supposed to have for Jesus to other people, things, and distractions, we rob Him of being able to be intimate with us. Our engagement with Christ must take precedence over everything else. How do you get complete in Jesus? Something powerful in your life is going to have to happen. Oneness requires action on your part. If a couple will be successful together, it's going to take the cooperation of both parties, not just one. There is a leader. In your relationship with Christ, Jesus is the leader. Jesus, left His entire genealogy and His biography here on Earth for you to review. You are here to simply make a choice from day to day.

In order for a pair to be one, they have to walk together with Jesus in the lead. This means you walk together according to the Word He set before you, and you are to delight in this Word day and night.

For how can two walk together unless they both agree? If two cannot walk together, they will come apart. For a house divided against itself cannot stand. Woman of God, your temple (your body) will fall into the snare of sin when it is not in agreement with the Holy Word of God. You can fall into lust, anger, malice, drunkenness and more simply because you decided that you were not going to be in agreement with the One who loves you more than anything in this world.

The Lord of Hosts Is Your Husband

If you don't delight in the Word of the Lord (your spiritual Husband), your wicked heart may choose to rebel against Him in Heaven, and trust me, He isn't having it. You've had all this time here on Earth to read the manual (Bible) that teaches you how to be His wife before you arrive at His home. You are without excuse.

B – Basic

I – Instructions

B – Before

L - Leaving

E – Earth

You Are a Wife in Training

Your position as wife, before anything else, is to be a servant. When you get to heaven, you will either be a "good and faithful" servant, or you will be a wicked servant. The High Priest of our calling will not have a wicked wife for Himself. He will not have a Priestess who has an unrepentant record of lewd conduct. If He could not trust her to be holy and rule on earth, how can He trust her to rule in Heaven? God has faith in you and He is faithful to you. This is your only opportunity to prove your faithfulness to Him.

Working Out Your Relationship

There is no such thing as an easy relationship with anybody. A relationship is a journey of two people. My relationship with Jesus Christ was the most difficult relationship I have ever been in in my entire life! Why? I had my own way that I wanted to go. I had my own way of doing things. When I signed up to accept Jesus Christ into my life, I didn't fully understand, at nine years old, that I was signing up to follow His path of life. After all, it's only His road, the road less traveled, that leads to eternal life. I repeatedly backslid, unable to fully grasp that I actually had to follow and obey God if I wanted to make it to heaven. I believed that once I was saved, I was always saved. This is one of the biggest lies that many of today's ministers have told people in order to get them to join their churches. Of course, nobody wants to go to hell, so they will gladly accept Jesus with their mouths.

They may even reserve a small spot for Him in their hearts. Whenever someone tells you that you will always have a place in their hearts, it is very likely that the person is not going to have a close relationship with you. As a matter of fact, what they are really saying is "Goodbye! I will think of you from time to time!" How many times have we done this to Jesus? I've walked away tons of times, and do you know what Jesus did? He walked right with me so He could see what I was doing. And then, He removed whatever I was following out of my life so I would get a very important message. I was to follow Him if I wanted to be with Him, and not the other way around. When I was married, I tried to control the direction of my relationship with my then husband. I believed that the path I'd created in the marriage would lead both of us to the Lord. I was determined to have an adultery free, safe, honest and prosperous marriage. As I was going towards Christ, I wanted my ex-husband to go in that direction with me. But He went in the opposite direction. Why? Because he wasn't the one leading. As a man, he wanted to be the one in the lead, even if it was to a dead end. He didn't follow the word of God. He followed the lust of his flesh, and ultimately, this led to the destruction of our marriage. He fought against me rigorously to ensure he would have his way, even if it cost me my life. It is God's will and proper order that the husband lead the marriage. That's the way He designed men. This is a perfect example of why we cannot afford to be unequally yoked with unbelievers.

I used this example to demonstrate that if we don't follow the instructions and directions of Jesus Christ as outlined for us in His Word, we greatly risk losing our relationships with Him for all of eternity.

I pray you understand that from day to day, your relationship with Jesus Christ is either growing or dwindling. This is the reason it is so important for you to give Jesus your time. One of the best ways to give the Lord your time is to give Him your entire life and everything you've got.

Relationship Killers

Ask yourself the following questions to identify gaps that may be dividing your relationship with Jesus Christ.

How much time do you spend alone with the Lord daily? How many distractions are interrupting the things you'd like to do for God while you are here on this Earth?

Does it appear that the Spirit of the Lord is heading in a completely different direction than some of the relationships you are pursuing? (Note: Where the Spirit of the Lord does not have precedence, lust is lurking).

Do you keep looking back at your past while Jesus waits for you? Are you still mourning over people places and situations that He has delivered you from?

When you have a bunch of relationship killers floating around in your life, it's easy for the doors of idolatry and adultery to be open. It also makes intimacy with God incredibly difficult. If you've noticed that your relationship with Jesus has holes in it, then it is time to work like never before to repair that relationship. Jesus is coming back very soon to claim His spotless bride.

Below are ways that we can have a better relationship with Christ.

Increase your faith – Increase your faith in who God is and what He is able to do in your life. Increase your faith in His love, care, and provision for you.

Learn to trust – When we don't trust someone, your relationship with them won't be successful. Until there is trust, you really don't have a relationship.

Learn to submit to holiness – We must submit to God before we submit to any man on this Earth. We must submit to God before we submit to church leadership, an employer or a husband. God doesn't want to control us. Submission is not a form of control. It's important to remember that a position of submission is a position where His holy power can mightily work through us.

Forsake all others – There are men who will walk in your life as counterfeits of Christ. The only man you are to submit to, other that Jesus Christ, is the one He has pointed out to be your God ordained husband. All others are looking for ways to use the power God placed on the inside of you for themselves before your husband can benefit from it.

Pray with strategic purpose – God is not a genie. He is more interested in developing your character than He is in enlarging your pocket book. Jesus told us that God knows everything we need before we ask, so there is a manner in which we are supposed to pray.

First, give honor to the Heavenly Father before entering prayer and when exiting prayer.

Second, glorify the name of the Lord.

Ask for His reign in your entire life that day.

Declare His will be done in your life.

State your allegiance with Heaven.

Humbly ask God to feed your desire for Him.

Humbly ask God to forgive you for your sins. This is important because we sin even when we are not trying to.

Release those in the spirit who have wronged you. Tell God you are forgiving them to be closer to Him.

Ask God to lead you on the paths you are to take today and guide you away from the paths of evil.

Profess that what is on the inside of you totally belongs to God today and for all of eternity.

Note: Praying in this manner is to pray in the manner that Jesus prayed when He went before the Lord. Some people repeat this prayer Word for Word. However, your most powerful prayers are the ones that come from within the depths of your heart and not the religions repetitions we often pray for the sake of praying.

After praying in this manner from day to day while alone with God, you should find yourself suited up and fully equipped for your walk with Christ.

Think of it this way. The only days that count in a couple's marriage are the days that they walk together in agreement. Every day that they walk together in love and faithfulness builds a stronger foundation for their marriage. Jesus stated that those who hear His words and don't obey them are like those who build their houses upon the sand. And when the wind and the waves beat upon that house, the house would be destroyed. But those who hear His Words and do not obey them are like those who build their houses upon a rock. And in the day of trouble, that house will stand.

What you put out in your engagement to Jesus will be reciprocated through the Holy Spirit's interaction with you. You'll also begin to walk in a realm fit for who you are in the

Lord. Intimacy is vital growing strong in the spirit. Rising early is necessary. Turning off our phones is a must. Seeking His face before social media is an <u>absolute must</u>. Turning off music you know doesn't glorify Him is mandatory.

To be one with Christ, you have to be in agreement with Him through His Word, and in your life. You have to be continuously walking with Him. You have to continuously let Him operate through you. To be one with Christ, you must continue to dedicate your gifts and talents to enlarge His Kingdom, and most importantly, you must have intimacy with Him. How much time do you spend per day being intimate with Jesus through prayer, praise, and worship? You have to know how to touch somebody without really touching them, and you can start with Jesus Christ.

Chapter 4

Your Calling to Priesthood

The Royal Priestess

We live in a time where every believer is required to preach the gospel, and not just preach the gospel, but be effective at living it. God isn't freely giving us the rewards of heaven. No... It's going to cost us something. We must make our communications with Jesus, our desires to do the will of God and our dedications to lives of obedience and holiness our top priorities every day. There is absolutely nothing more important than our allegiance to Jesus Christ.

When you are in full agreement with Jesus, it is then that He can cleanse, heal, cover and make you whole as you continue with Him. Nevertheless, He is coming back soon and you don't have much time to get things right. Don't be foolish.

Keep your Bible open, pray and get the fullness of God's anointing for your life every single day. Worship is when you are actively carrying your cross, walking in His direction, and away from the ungodly paths. True worship is the worship that breaks every chain of bondage formed by the enemy.

A Perfect Presentation

As a Royal Priestess, you are a temple for God to pour His Spirit in. It's the Lord desire that you'd be a consecrated vessel to be filled with spiritual things. As a Priestess, whether you accept you're calling or not, you will pour out whatever you have in you. You will pour out your knowledge upon every single soul you touch. The Almighty God will smell and measure what you pour out, so it is very important that we live our lives responsibly. It is important that we continue walking in the beauty of holiness and grasping the opportunities that God has given us. It's important that we are not a stench to Gods' nostrils with sin.

Being a person who lived with rejection the majority of my life, I've never desired to be a minister. To be honest, I didn't think I was good enough. Even though God would give me strong messages and dreams when I was young, I didn't speak about my visions in church. I wasn't the type of person a pastor would look at and see any remnant of promise. There was a point when God had spoken to me through an Apostle, who said that I would be able to prophecy to people one day. All I had to do was give God six months of my time. At the time, I was so distracted by my desires to please my boyfriend that I had trouble giving God more than two days of consistency. Like most people who sit in the pews of church, I would sometimes sit in my seat and secretly say in my heart:

"I wish my pastor would give me the mic."

"I wish my pastor would call on me to speak. I know I have something to say that would greatly enhance the kingdom of God!"

"I wish God would speak to my Pastor and let him know that I am the next great leader in this church!"

Week after week and year after year, nothing like that ever happened. I would sit in the pews desiring to do the work of God, but I didn't have any training or any knowledge of how or where I'd go to get trained. It appeared that that the only office of servitude that was available to me was being a hostess. And I am not really a person suited to be a hostess. When I feel the Holy Spirit wanting to get something great out of me, I am ready to go!

Set Apart

In chapter one, I talked about how God divorced me from my husband. Most people might say, "But God hates divorce!" Yes, God does hate divorce, but He also allows it. Not only does He allow it, He has done it Himself to his own people. God may even call for it so that His people can be purified. When I was married I didn't understand that my marriage was a complete fraud according to the Word of God. God loves us so much that He would never sentence those who love Him to a lifetime of hell on earth. The Bible states in Exodus 21:10-11 that it is a husband's responsibility (even if he is unfaithful) to provide clothing, food and the rights of his wife should not diminish. If he doesn't, she has the right to be released.

My husband kept me so poor that I had no money, no secure housing, no clothes to wear and I had holes in the back of my only shoes. The Bible also states in 1 Corinthians 7:15 that if an unbelieving spouse leaves the marriage, the believing spouse is not under bondage. My ex-husband never physically left the house because, of course, the thing he desired the most (sex) was residing there. But he did not provide for his household. Additionally, he didn't separate from his parents so we could be one flesh. He claimed he was at his mom's house every single day before he came home to me. Before I saw him, he had already eaten, his financial issues were handled by his grandmother, and his clothing had been washed by his mom. Being married to me was a complete and utter joke to him. It took me a long time to really accept that the moment my husband set his heart to abuse me financially, emotionally, physically, mentally and sexually, he had already left home. Even when I realized this, I strongly wanted confirmation from God before I set him free. Once reality set in, I became so enraged that I left our home for several days, and it was then that God freed me from that marriage to save both of our lives.

During the time I was away, I was desperately seeking the voice of God. I was full of a murderous spirit, and that spirit tormented me night and day. One night, I was walking down the street in my last and only pair of jeans. Those jeans were worn out and ripped from my inner thigh. It was 9:30 in the evening, and I had just come back from purchasing new jeans from Forever 21 when I was met on the street by a prophet. He was trying to get to a prayer meeting, and apparently, his bus was late. When he began to speak, I was so angry that I wouldn't face him. I thought to myself, "If this is a false prophet, I will strike him down immediately. Let him speak one false word!" *Yeah... it was that bad.* I had become very angry in my heart because of false prophets I'd encountered in my past stole my money and spoke false words over me. In my state of mind, I just couldn't take it anymore. The young prophet, sensing my anger, made a bold move and gently stepped around me to face me. As he continued to speak, all of the anger I felt began to flood away and that anger was replaced by the peace of God. The prophet told me that there was a nation of women waiting to hear from me. He said that I would speak to them about abuse, neglect, rape and other things. He said that the wisdom of God was always in me, but when I was younger and tried to give women advice, they would never listen. He said the words that were coming from me were of God. He said that the relationship that I was in, God said, "That's not it." The prophet gave me details about the husband God has in mind for me. God spoke through the young prophet and said my husband would love me, appreciate me, and most importantly, he would not lie to me. Ministry was a requirement for the marriage that God had in mind. Once I was in ministry, my husband would recognize me and that we would know each other by the spirit.

I had been one of those people who ran from God for years because I didn't believe there was any real benefit in serving Him. All I'd ever experienced in my life was hurt, pain and disappointment. Over the years, when God would show me end-time dreams and visions of things to come, those visions made me really not want much to do with Him. The things I saw were so horrific and frightening at times that they made me feel hopeless and more alone than ever. Regardless of how hard I worked to run away and escape the calling of God in my life, God had divinely appointed a time and place for His prophetic mouthpiece to find me and say to me, "You are one of those people who don't have a choice but to go into ministry!" I thought to myself, "Why won't God leave me alone? Why would God want to use a loser like me? I've just lost my family and every tiny thing I loved. Why would I, of all people, have to do ministry?" I didn't believe, at the time, that I was equipped, popular enough, pretty enough or worthy enough to be used by God. Knowing my thoughts, God spoke through the prophet and said, "God is going to restore your self-worth and self-esteem supernaturally, but you have to go to Him. All this time God hasn't allowed anyone to help you because He wants to be the one to help you. God is jealous over you." While everything he spoke gave me a sense of peace and the confirmation I needed to file for divorce, I was kept wondering why anyone would even consider listening to me! I didn't think I had anything to say.

I look back on that moment now and chuckle to myself because today, I am in the process of completing four books, all the while, running two blogs and an online ministry. I ran from God for a while, but eventually, I answered the call on my life.

What God knew was that my story, God's guidance and the wisdom of the Holy Spirit would go forth to change the hearts of His daughters in many places. I didn't know what I was going to say at first, but whenever God placed me before someone who needed help, I was able to draw from my file drawer of experience to be a blessing to that person. It wasn't me. It was the power and grace of God within me that produced words powerful enough to reach women from all walks of life. I'd forgotten that throughout the bible, God used those people who were the least and called them to the forefront. And from there, He used them to lead His people to victory.

My question is to you, will you answer the call God has on your life? Another woman desperately needs to know your testimony. Another young girl desperately needs to see the evidence of God's love, and your testimony will serve as a bridge to help her get past her tests. My story is just one of the millions of examples of how God calls His people, even when they are still in darkness. So yes, you can bask in his promise to secure a future for you. In God's divinely inspired love letter to you, He called you a generation within yourself. His desire is that you be holy because He is holy. When His loving eyes behold you, He sees you as the royalty you are. Your story of brokenness and your survival is your testimony to the world that you've been redeemed by the blood of the Lamb. God is willing to restore you because He wants you to restore others. When God calls you into His fold, He has called you to ministry. Whether you are afraid to move forward or not, God is still requiring you to go to work!

Many will say they don't know which areas of ministry they are called to, and while this might be true for some of you, it is not a justifiable excuse for not moving forward in the Lord.

In early 2014, the Lord gave me a very moving dream. In the dream, I saw myself ministering to a woman in China. The woman was Chinese, of course, and she was sitting on a brick wall crying uncontrollably as I read the Bible to her. She looked into my eyes and said to me, *"Nobody ever told me that God could use me. Nobody ever told me that God had called me to leadership."* This beautiful, educated, kind-hearted woman of God had been in church her whole life and nobody had mentored her, called her out or helped equip her for the work of the Lord. All of her life, she'd believed that she wasn't of any use to God, other than being a church member and giving money to the church. She'd never considered that God had given her a higher position in His Kingdom than the one she was accustomed to serving in. You see, God said in His Word that she was a minister of the Lord, but nobody ever pointed it out to her. In all those years she'd spent in church, she thought that she was useless.

Held To the Highest Standard

Being a minister or priest of the Lord is a very beautiful thing. One very important thing that the Lord also pointed out in the dream was that many believers of Jesus Christ also believe they can completely get away with unholy acts like fornication, clubbing, drinking and doing drugs because they have not been informed that according to the Word, they are Priests of God. They have said in their hearts, "I can do whatsoever I want because I'm just a Christian. I'm not perfect. It's not like I'm a priest. Only the priests have to keep themselves pure! No matter what I do, as long as I tell God I'm sorry, I'm still getting into heaven." After all, many people understand that God is holding the priests to a higher standard than the rest. In response to the wicked speech in the heart of His people, God has said, "Not so!"

He has called us all to be priests, and when we all stand before Him on the great Day of Judgment, He will hold everyone who professed to be believers to the standard of priest, and nothing less. In His Word, He has called every believer a priest!

Many will say that they don't know the first thing about being a priestess, but the truth is if you know about Jesus, you can better understand the calling of priesthood by following in His footsteps. In truth, the priesthood of Christ is holy discipleship and servitude. Below are some of the ways those who are called by Him are to follow in His footsteps:

1. Know the Word. It's important that we study the Word of God to show ourselves approved by God. You should be in God's Word a minimum of 45 minutes a day.

2. Obey all the commandments of God. The Word states that in Matthew 5:19, "Whosoever, therefore, shall break one of these least commandments, and shall teach men so, he shall be called the least in the kingdom of heaven: but whosoever shall do and

teach *them*, the same shall be called great in the kingdom of heaven."

3. Address the Father with reverence and keep His name holy. Always honor the name of the Lord, and do not take it in vain. We are not to place God's name in the same category as profanity. We are to claim that we are Christian and not model our lives after Christ.

4. Be in the world but not of it. This, in itself, is a process of releasing the things that are common to us. We can't hide from the world, but we shouldn't act like it either. Most importantly, we shouldn't look like it.

5. Keep your mind on the things of heaven and not the things of this world. This world is only temporary. Our time in this world is temporary. Eternity is a very long time.

6. Allow God's Holy Spirit to order your footsteps. God is always giving orders, detailing what we are to

tackle on the day at hand. It's important that we are focused on the things that He wants.

7. Keep yourself pure and unpolluted. Consecration is so important. Because we are priests, we are not to keep company with people who say they are believers but continue to walk in darkness.

8. Bridle your tongue. Life and death are in the power of the tongue. Blessing and cursing should not flow out of the same fountain. For the Lord has said that if we are neither hot nor cold, we will be lukewarm, and He will spew us out of his mouth.

9. Check yourself to see if you have produced the offspring of being intimate with the Spirit of God. God says that in our positions, we are to produce fruit, and not just any fruit, but the fruit of the Holy Spirit. Every tree not bearing good fruit will be cut down and thrown into the fire.

10. Feed the hungry, heal the sick, and cleanse the lepers. The truth is, we can't do this if we don't have the genuine love and fullness of Jesus in our lives.

11. Evangelize. Tell people about Jesus Christ. Jesus said in Mark 8:38, "Whosoever, therefore, shall be ashamed of me and of my words in this adulterous and sinful generation; of him also shall the Son of man be ashamed, when he cometh in the glory of his Father with the holy angels." God has given us a lot of talents to spread the gospel with. There are many people who have been elevated because of their talents, but they've never given God the glory, acting as if the talents were their own. God wants us to be a light to the world, not vessels of darkness. If God has given you a talent, take that talent and dedicate it back to Him and give Him a full return on His investment. God doesn't need your money. More than anything, He wants souls. He has already purchased them with the blood of His Son, Jesus Christ.

Apostle Paul stated that we could do all of these things, and if we have not love, we are as clanging brass. It's no secret that this world can be rather cold and dark. The injustices we face in our lives can plant seeds of bitterness in our hearts and choke out the love that is supposed to be flowing from us to God's people. This is why intimacy with Jesus is so important. There is something wonderful about being in a fulfilling relationship with someone who brings out the absolute best in you. Where there is love, there is power. And love is the catalyst for the healing power of the Holy Spirit to flow from your life into the lives of others if you are going to be an effective minister of the gospel, love has to absolutely lead the way.

Praying Gods Will

"Thy kingdom come. Thy will be done. On Earth as it is in Heaven." Our High Priest prayed this prayer to help us better understand God's plans for us, and this prayer is one of the most effective prayers that we can pray.

Truth be told, we all have a responsibility to be actively working in the Kingdom of God. What this means is that we are working in such a way that the power of God is brought to Earth through us.

Is God getting the glory for your life? If not, it's likely because

1. You haven't fully surrendered it to Him.

2. You don't have faith in Him.

3. You have not partnered with Him in obedience.

4. You keep leaving the door open for adultery and fornication.

Getting Healing Before Ministry

Remember, that God called you out of darkness into His marvelous light. He called you out of fear. He called you out of danger. He called you out of poverty. He called you out of deception. He called you out of bondage...period. The Lord desires you to be able to bask in the light of His Holy presence all the days of your life, and in His presence is the power to restore you.

Have you ever heard the expression, "Hurt people, hurt people"? It's incredibly true. Hurt people are selfish people and not selfless people. Of course, hurt people can love someone whose love they think will heal their souls and benefit their lives. Nevertheless, it's very difficult for hurt people to love anyone who seriously needs them to be more than what they have to offer. And people who are deeply in need of other people are often seriously hurting themselves. Walking in the divinely ordained role of priestess means walking in wholeness and holiness. Yes, we will have our ups and downs in life, but it is our responsibility to make sure that what we suffer in the realm of the earth does not interfere with the higher Heavenly calling of God on our lives.

Cleansing the Temple

Ladies, the high calling we have to answer to is a great and honorable calling. Before you begin to take on a new mindset to tackle the issues in your lives, you should go further than just asking yourself, "What would Jesus do?" You should ask yourself, "Is my holy High Priest of a Husband in agreement with this place, service, outfit, music, food choice, my romantic interest, emotions and my attitude? Is my temple prepared for His arrival? Is my temple clean and pure enough for His use?"

Asking yourself these questions will help you see the differences between the wise virgin and the foolish virgin. If you remember the parable in Mathew 25, all of the virgins were waiting on Jesus, but only half of the virgins present were ready for His arrival. Not too long ago, the Lord demonstrated His return in one of my dreams. He showed up in the sky and passed by swiftly. When I and others saw Him going by, we began to pray in the spirit. We wanted to increase our anointing (oil) so He would recognize us, but by the time He came, it was too late. Jesus had come and gone, and I was not taken with Him. Matthew Chapter 25, helped me to understand my dream.

Matthew 25:1-13 (KJV) Then shall the kingdom of heaven be likened unto ten virgins, which took their lamps, and went forth to meet the bridegroom. And five of them were wise, and five were foolish. <u>They that were foolish took their lamps, and took no oil with them:</u> But the wise took oil in their vessels with their lamps. While the bridegroom tarried, they all slumbered and slept. And at midnight there was a cry made, Behold, the bridegroom cometh; go ye out to meet him. Then all those virgins arose, and trimmed their lamps. And the foolish said unto the wise, "<u>Give us of your oil; for our lamps are gone out</u>". But the wise answered, saying, Not so; lest there be not enough for us and you: but go ye rather to them that sell, and buy for yourselves. And while *they went to buy, the bridegroom came; and they that were ready went in with him to the marriage: and the door was shut. Afterward came also the other virgins, saying, Lord, Lord, open to us. But he answered and said, Verily I say unto you, I know you not. Watch, therefore, for ye know neither the day nor the hour wherein the Son of man cometh.*

Now that you've confirmed that you have been called to ministry, it is important for you to answer this call. It is your job be one of God's royal ambassadors in the Earth, keep yourself pure, and not add to the pollution and evil works of the devil. You cannot be a holy priestess of God and work the seductive manipulative ways of Jezebel for the sake of advancing your personal agenda. If you turn to seduction or sin, God will turn you away from His gates and say, "I never knew you."

All too often, women are willing to be attached to the yokes and carry the burdens of men who can't do anything for them, but Jesus gives us everything we need, and He promises that His yoke is easy and His burden is light. The enemy cannot go the heights Jesus will take you. Stay in forgiveness so that love (the catalyst for receiving the anointing of the Holy Spirit) can catapult your life. When you are thinking back on the men who've hurt you, remember that they were very likely nothing more than satanic bait designed to get you out of the will of God. When you stop looking at the devil's bait and begin looking to the light of Jesus Christ, you will get free and healed. Are you ready to commit to a life of serving Jesus Christ?

If you're ready to submit to God's work, pray the following:

Heavenly Father, thank you for all of the mercy You have shown me all the days of my life. Lord, I pray that You continue to reign in my life. I pray the things You speak in Heaven will divinely touch my ears and quicken me to perform Your works in the Earth. Lord, I pray that Your will for my life would supersede every other plan already in the works for my life. Lord, I ask that You empower and sharpen me daily so that I am effective in spreading the gospel of Jesus Christ to men and women everywhere. I asked that You will forgive me for my sins, mindsets, and habits that don't please You or bring the glory Your Holy name deserves. I am wholeheartedly changing my heart today, Lord. I'm changing to because I want more of You. I am changing because I love You. I am changing because I want to spend eternity with You. Jesus, I ask that You come into my heart today. I believe that You gave Your life on the cross just for me. I believe that You died on the cross, took the keys from Hell and Death, rose again, and ascended to Heaven. Lord, I thank You for what You have done to save my soul. Lord, I commit my spirit to be one with You. I promise to lay down all my sins and let go of every wicked influence that inspires me to commit sin. Lord, I promise to take delight in Your instructions for my life day and night and esteem Your will above all others. Take my heart, Jesus. I give it to You today. In Jesus name, I pray... Amen.

If you have prayed that prayer, you have invited the salvation provided to us through Jesus Christ into your life. From this day forward, you are to walk upright before the Lord.

Chapter 5

Keeping Your Purity

When God prophetically freed me from my marriage and I convinced my ex to sign the divorce papers, I knew God had changed my life for better, but I wasn't transformed. And I certainly wasn't whole either. I was looking everywhere and wondering when God would finally send me the man He said would love, appreciate and never lie to me. I was incredibly lonely, vulnerable and I had a mindset that still wasn't pleasing to Him. Because I wasn't having sex, I told myself that I could compromise in other ways once I located the right person. For one, I didn't believe that any man would stay with a woman, be happy with that woman or be around any woman who refused to please him sexually. After all... MEN HAVE NEEDS! And secondly, I HAD NEEDS! At that point, I couldn't fathom the idea that

God would require me to be one hundred percent faithful to Him. The idea of walking in holiness was beyond my range of thinking. I thought sexting was okay. I thought kissing and foreplay were both okay... as long as I didn't actually have sex. At that point, I also began to reason in my mind that maybe my husband didn't love me enough because I wasn't sexy enough. I had gained a lot of weight from all the emotional eating I did in our marriage, and I didn't look anything like the woman he'd once said was his ideal woman. At the time, I believed my ex's ideal woman was someone who was gorgeous, curvaceous, extremely sexual, seductive, and most importantly, submissive.

He would go to strip clubs, and then, brag to his friends about how wonderful the other women were. Whenever he cheated, he would brag to his friends about his affairs, and they would all cheer him on. I longed deeply for some person, somewhere to tell him, "Hey man! That's wrong. Go home and be with your wife. She loves you." I knew I could never compare to those women in his eyes, but in God's eyes, they couldn't hold a candle to me.

Once we'd separated, I told myself, "No man will ever leave me again simply because I can't do the things he wants me to do." Pop culture had convinced me that I had to walk around looking like a diva in order to earn the respect of men, especially black men. Pop culture sent the message that women worthy of diamond rings had to have it all. Their weave had to be 22 inches long. They needed butt injections. Their waist had to be 12 inches smaller than their hips. Pop culture sent the message that not only should a wife resemble a highly paid stripper, she should also know how to dance like one to ensure that her husband never left home. I didn't know that God had a different route for me to get to a place of love and happiness.

So what did I do? I starved myself to lose 30 pounds. I went on a crazy diet that consisted of me eating next to nothing. I desperately wanted the approval of men. I got a new job to support myself, and one of my co-workers just happened to be a professional pole dancing instructor. When I told her that I wanted her to teach me how to pole dance, she agreed to help me. So, I decided I would take a few weeks to prepare for the class. I wanted to become more flexible and decrease the risk of injuring myself. My goal was to first learn how to do the splits. I even felt I could learn to twerk a little better. I searched YouTube and I found videos that would teach me how to be a more sensual dancer and prep my body for pole dancing. I was dedicated to doing the only thing I knew how to do: be sexual. I wanted to make sure my future husband would consider me to be a blessing from God and cherish me. During that time, I learned a lot, and I thought that it was God's will for me to be a sexual goddess to my husband.

One evening after I'd gotten back home from a date, I laid down to go to sleep. I'd spent the evening trying to bring my date to know to Jesus Christ. When I ministered the gospel to him, he became furious with me and claimed that

Christianity was "the white man's religion." I didn't argue with him, but he was so angry that he ripped me to shreds with his words. As I tried to forget his words and drift off to sleep, I began to have a very demonic nightmare. The demons were telling me to leave him alone and that he belonged to them. When I tried to wake up, I couldn't. I felt paralyzed and the demonic forces began to attack my mind. Eventually, I was able to wake myself up, but just as I opened my eyes, I saw a small demon walk across my room and go into hiding. Demonic attacks like this were a very common part of my life because of the calling God had on me. I was very afraid, but I prayed and asked God to surround me with His fire of protection. Normally, that particular prayer worked and stopped many demonic attacks. But this time, it did not work. I went back to sleep and the demons began to attack my mind with more force than they'd attacked it before. I could sense them telling me that they had the legal right to be there. (For those of you who are not familiar with spiritual warfare, there is no excuse for you to be ignorant to it. Do your research. Equip yourself with the knowledge you need to be a successful prayer warrior). I asked myself what I was doing that gave them the power or right to be here. Why were they getting stronger, despite my prayers? As I looked beside my bed, I saw my computer, and that's when it hit me. It was what I had on my computer that gave them access to me. I had downloaded several of the videos I was using to learn pole dancing to my hard drive of my computer. I did this so I wouldn't have to connect to the internet when I watched them. Honestly, I did not want to get rid of those videos. My desire to be some man's dream woman was attached to what I was learning in those videos, nevertheless, I felt the Spirit of the Lord urging me to let them go. At that point, I had no idea why He wanted me to delete the videos, but I knew I had to obey Him. Disappointed, I deleted the pole dancing videos one by one. Once I was done, I shut down my laptop and prayed again against the demons that were attacking me in my sleep. When I was done, I felt the Holy Spirit tell me, "Not everything is fit for the saints." That could only mean one thing. The man God has for me is holy and there is no way he would require his wife to act like a seductress. Relieved, I went back to sleep and I didn't suffer through any more attacks that night. The doors that gave the devil access to me were now closed.

Several months later, I discussed the incident with someone I trusted in the faith. They explained to me that pole dancing was satanic in nature and that in ancient Babylonian days, it was a form of Baal worship. The pole itself was in the form of an idol, and it represented the male penis. Going around the pole sensually and preforming sexual acts opened portals for demons. Whenever Satan wants to accomplish mass deception and open doors for demonic infiltration, his primary tactic is to sexually charge the atmosphere. As a matter of fact, a large part of the Bible covers the issue of the stripper pole, but many don't see this topic because it's hidden.

The Gospel & the Stripper Pole

For those who are curious about the Biblical references to ancient Babylon, Baal, and pole dancing, the Lord makes reference to these points in Judges 16:25 (and 40 other places).

In many translations, the word "grove" is referred to as "Asherah pole" or "idol pole." The goddess Asherah was presented as a consort to Baal. **Worship of Asherah was primarily noted for its sensuality and the male and female prostitution that was done around the altar of poles.** *King Solomon (who had seven hundred wives and three hundred concubines) worshiped Asherah, along with other idols. Queen Jezebel didn't just worship Asherah, but she established over four hundred prophets under Asherah. These poles were always on the side of the altars. There are many mentions of this in the Old Testament. Be sure to conduct your own research about what was happening during that time. Also notice* *that the Bible states that those poles were "erected", and they were in high places. The children of Israel were supposed to reject the poles of Asherah, but why didn't they? Why did God have to keep fighting His children to stop their involvement in temple prostitution and idol worship around these erected poles? Something must have drawn them to the pole. Now today, this wooden pole or temple of poles has evolved and is now in places like studios, gyms, strip clubs, playgrounds and even churches, and the spirit of Jezebel is still rampant in the church. Christ has to come before everything in our lives. This includes fitness and our attempts to obtain or seduce men (including our husbands).*

Let's face it. Hearing the call to repentance can sometimes be the largest punch to our ego and the biggest blow to our pride, but it's the only call in the world that keeps us away from hell's fire. So many people have decided not to walk the way of the Lord or to walk wayward with the Lord, but the way to Christ is a straight and narrow path. There simply is no exception to this rule. As Christians, we can often find ourselves pointing our fingers at pastors and ministry leaders who have been caught in scandals like adultery, homosexuality and stealing from the church. We find ourselves saying things like, "Shame on them! They were supposed to protect the sheep! They are priests! We trusted them!" Are we to judge them? Absolutely! The Bible states that as members of the Body of Christ, we are to judge those who are inside of the church. It's our right and our responsibility. However, there is something very important you need to catch. In the previous chapter, we talked about how God called you to priesthood. And the Lord can say the same thing to you on the Day of Judgment.

Imagine standing before the Lord and God calls your name on the judgment floor of heaven. He looks at your record and sees all the sins you committed when you were in Christ, and He says to you, "I was trusting you. I gave you the right to become a part of My family when you didn't deserve it. You seduced the men I sent you to. You fornicated with your brothers. I was trusting you to be a holy vessel within My sanctuary. I gave you the position of a priest when I called you into my Kingdom, but you tainted your robe every chance you got! Didn't My Word state, "Be ye holy for I am holy?" Please remember that God is not holding us to any standard less than the standard of a priest, and the standard of a priest is one of holiness.

We must understand that God has called each and every one of the saints adopted as sons and daughters of the Royal Priesthood to purity, and not because He wants us to be bored in life (That's what Satan wants us to believe). God calls us to purity because He wants us to be shining lights in this dark world.

How can we be anointed vessels of light if we are going around spreading the darkness in us, all while, using the name of Jesus? How can we claim that Jesus is our Lord and Savior if we are in complete bondage to sin? If we are in bondage to sin, our testimonies before the lost are complete lies. Hence, we are hypocrites.

There are several things that God wants to bring to your attention regarding purity.

God has called you to be a priest

God is requiring you to be whole.

God is requiring you to be pure.

God is requiring you to be a light.

God is expecting you to be a vessel that spreads love, purity, and light to the world.

When we disobey God, we have left our posts and abandoned our royal positions in the Lord's Kingdom. At that point, anything we do for God is polluted. When we don't keep our purity, we have allowed ourselves to be tools for Satan to pollute the very people God is trying to reach. Yes, Jesus can forgive us for these things when we truly repent, but you should know that the actions we have taken have serious consequences. The consequences of your actions aren't just suffered by you, but to the world and the generations to come will pay for your choices.

Consider the very first human relationship recorded: the relationship between Adam and Eve. Eve listened to the suggestions of Satan and caused Adam to fall, and this fall led to separation from the blessings of God for every generation of humanity.

Having a Plan

Hopefully, at this point, you've come to recognize just how important purity is to your walk. Purity isn't just a state of being that we can reach instantly, but it requires a process to get to. Once we've gone through the process of reaching purity, we have to have an action plan to maintain our purity so that we can meet the standard of our high calling in Jesus Christ.

Silencing the Enemy

One of the first things you will want to do to maintain your purity in the Lord is silence the enemy. Before Jesus got ready to move into ministry, He went to a place where He could be alone. He moved away from all influence, and when Satan approached Him with suggestions, He rebuked him with the Word. Nothing was more important to Jesus than doing the will of the Father. Just as nothing should be more important to us than doing the will of the Father.

It's vital that we silence the voices around us. The voices of music, the voices of media and the voices of people who don't support our walks with Christ. Every voice you hear is ministering something to you. You absolutely have to consider what the music you are listening to on a day to day basis is ministering to you. If I turn on the radio now, especially if it's an R&B or Hip Hop station, 97% percent of the songs are about sex and ways to sexually manipulate someone's mind, body, and soul. Some of those songs are literally having sex with our minds. Keeping this type of garbage on while you are trying to live for God will make your walk a lot harder than it has to be. If your music, the shows you watch and the literature you read is ministering or suggesting sin to you, it's time to put it away.

Some of the things today's media ministers to us include:

Suggestions that fornication is acceptable.

Easy access to pornography through fashion advertisements.

Disrespect for other human beings by suggesting that others are lower than us.

The idea that it's okay to blaspheme the name of Jesus and walk around with full of pride, so we don't walk with the love of God.

The demonic revelations of horoscopes which lead to witchcraft curses over our lives.

Ways to hate our bodies so that we will fit an unrealistic, digitally created idea of human perfection. The only way we can obtain these unrealistic standards in life is through starving ourselves, drugs, cutting ourselves up and injecting foreign substances into our bodies. Our bodies are not our own. They are the temples of God. We are God's masterpieces.

When we don't shut the door on these types of worldly ministries, we keep the door open for the enemy's suggestions. No... we will never be able to completely silence him, but we can certainly tone down all the things he bombards us with so we can keep our focus on the will of the Lord and His still small voice.

Separating From the Enemy

The second thing we must do is separate ourselves from the enemy. Sometimes, the enemy is your boyfriend. Sometimes, the enemy is your husband. Sometimes, your enemies are your closest friends, associates, or even your family members. To be sanctified means you are set apart. You have to remember that Jesus did not come to bring peace, but He came to bring a sword, and whosoever loves their mother, father, sister, or brother more than Him is not worthy of Him. The easiest way to identify your enemy is by recognizing people who intentionally try to lead you into sin. If they are continuously trying to drag you to clubs, even though they know you have turned your life around to follow Christ, it is time to let that person go. If you are dating or associating with men who do not respect or appreciate your walk of purity and are making attempts to get you into sin, you need to close the door on those relationships. Sometimes, God will close doors for you. The more you give up for God, the more He will bring you into His presence, and the more you are in His presence, the more intimate He will be with you. The more intimate you are with Him, the greater the anointing will be and the more the anointing will flow from you.

A few weeks before the Lord removed me from my previous marriage, He started letting me know that His presence was in my home. He was watching and waiting for something, but I didn't know exactly why He was visiting me. My ex had an obsession with vampire movies and television shows, so he would bring those demonic dvds into our home. One day, God told me, "No vampires in your home! I do not want you to watch the Twilight (part three) movie that is coming out. There is something very wrong with it. It is releasing something over the nation!" I agreed. If the God of all the universe could take the time out of His busy schedule to come and visit me in my raggedy, bunny cage, studio apartment, while I was living in a demon infested city just to bring me a message, then surely, I should listen to Him! Well... I delivered the message to my husband, and a day or two later, he suggested that we'd see Twilight! Needless to say, the anger of the Lord was kindled in me because of his dedication to rebelling against the King of Heaven and Earth. But I quickly let the anger go because I knew that the Lord was there and heard what my then husband had said. There was simply no reverence for God in his heart. Less than a month later, God took me away from him, and needless to say, he never repented.

Access Denied

When you are under the protection of Christ, nothing can get to you unless you remove your soul from under His protection. You may need to close several doors to make it difficult for the enemy to gain access to you. Below are examples of doors that you may need to close so the enemy doesn't have access.

The gateway of your eyes. The eyes are often referred to as windows, however, they are still an entry way. We need to be incredibly mindful of what type of things we allow our eyes to see. The mind, being carnal, will record the things that intrigue it the most and keep a permanent record. Sometimes, Satan will go and pull the old records from your mind and replay them to keep suggesting sin to you. We may not be able to erase the sinful images our minds have recorded in the past, but we can make sure that our future is not full of them. Just recently, I was using Facebook, and as I was scrolling down my news feed, a video began to play automatically. In the video was of an overweight transsexual man dancing lewdly on camera with no undergarments on. I quickly opted for the video to be removed from my feed so that I wouldn't see it again, but by that time, it was too late. The image was branded in my mind, and that night, the enemy was able to release a perverted dream to me because of what my eyes had seen. The very next day, I changed my Facebook account settings to prohibit videos from automatically playing so that I could better protect my temple.

The gateway of your ears. The ear is an instrument of the mind. We have to be mindful of what we allow ourselves to hear, especially in relation to music. Music records automatically in our minds, and some music has been satanically crafted to ensure that we never forget the message at hand. Another way that we can protect our ears is by distancing ourselves away from people who are speaking wickedness into our lives. One example of this is listening to a man who knows how to easily stimulate our largest sex organ (which happens to be our brains) with his words alone. As women of God, we should never allow ourselves to be entertained by seducing spirits. We also need to watch out for men who are speaking abusive words and lies to us. If he wouldn't speak those words in a pulpit at church, then he shouldn't be speaking that garbage into your temple. Things like trash talk scar our minds and cause us to believe that our value is diminished. When we are beaten down mentally, living lives of holiness becomes difficult because we begin to feel anything but whole. When we don't feel whole, we will easily subject ourselves to the devices of the enemy because our spiritual armor has been punctured. At that point, we're looking for spiritual medicine and may not care how we get it. A wounded spirit is likely to turn to sex, drugs, alcohol and looseness because the person no longer values himself or herself. If you are in an abusive or disrespectful situation with any person in your life, it is important that you find the strength you need in God to remove yourself from that relationship so you can be whole.

The gateway of the mouth. – Notice the Word of God says it's not what goes into a person's mouth that makes them unclean, but what comes out of it. Have you ever noticed that people who are drunk with alcohol, lust or anger say the most awful things? They are speaking into the atmosphere out of the carnality of their minds. By doing so, they are throwing a party for demons to get things jumping off in their lives. Your mouth can get you into a lot of trouble. Your mouth is a gateway of life and death. A man knows how far he can go with you at any given moment because of what you speak out of your mouth. The angels of the Lord also record all of the things that come out of your mouth. In your purity walk, if you find that your thoughts are impure, keep your mouth closed until you can speak or pray what the Holy Spirit desires you to say.

The gateway of our hands – Your hands are used to carry things from one location to another. You carry things in the spirit. You deliver messages from your mind when you type them, and you use them to establish relationships with people. With that being said, you need to be careful of who you touch and who you allow to touch you, especially in the church. Learn to keep your hands guarded so you are not affected spiritually. When using electronics as a way of communicating with people, one must be careful of the types of messages they are transferring from their hands. Your hands are supposed to be used for blessing people, not enticing people into sin. For example, using your hands for sexting or cybersex will open doorways that are no good for you or the person you are interacting with. We also have to be mindful of how we use our hands. Pornographic movies, raunchy books and sex toys should not be found in our hands. At the same time, you should not touch the genitals of another person, nor should you touch your own genitals with the purpose of receiving sexual gratification through masturbation or stimulation. Considering that man's bodies are indeed the temple of God, how dare we defile our bodies with the abusive things Satan has lined up for it. Pornography is temple abuse on camera. Masturbation is temple abuse in private. Foreplay or fondling a person you're not married to is corporate temple abuse. If you really love yourself and your neighbor, you won't do things that cause either of you to fall away from God.

The gateway of your sexual organs – In the Bible, God refers to a woman's womb as a matrix. Either light or darkness will be birthed out of it, depending on who we yield it to. The right touch of any of your sexual organs can cause a light switch to go off in your brain, making you completely blind to the light of God in that moment. Why risk falling back into the sin you are trying to get free from by giving someone any part of your body (which is the temple of the Lord) in such a way that tempts you to sin? The gateway of your sex organs is one that allows for a deeply planted stronghold. It allows for an illegal marriage to be created, a marriage that was not ordained by God. Secondly, the stronghold over you can reach every aspect of your life and your destiny. It can pollute your mind, your heart, your finances, your name, your well-being, your ministry and more. Lust doesn't just like to have fun and go away. It likes to have its fun and string you along for a never-ending ride. It will drag you through the mud it already has waiting for you. It seeks to do nothing but disgrace you in this life and eternity. The door of your sexual organs should always be closed and completely off limits to anybody who is not your God ordained spouse.

The gateway of your feet – Your feet take you places. The Bible says one thing that the Lord absolutely hates is "feet that are swift to run to trouble". Your feet can take you to a place of sin or they can take you to a place of righteousness.

Don't let your feet walk you, run you, peddle you or drive you to any place where there is an opportunity for temptation, as you are building yourself up in the Lord.

With all of these things noted, our action plan for purity should consist of ways to keep our gateways closed. With our hearts guarded and gateways closed, we can easily stay on the pathways of the Lord, and not be moved into the way of destruction.

Here are things that can be also be included in your action plan for purity.

Staying away from R-rated movies with violence, demons and sex scenes that include nudity.

Moving away from secular music that doesn't glorify God, but glorifies the works of the flesh only.

Refusing to watch TV programs that glorify sexual perversion and extreme violence.

Unsubscribing to friends or pages in your social media accounts that share pornographic images.

Keeping away from lukewarm believers. The Bible states that we are not to keep company with such people as they pollute the faith. (Know that God does make a distinction between the wicked and the righteous, not by the titles they profess, but by the actions, they take to actually follow Jesus Christ).

Get involved in a ministry that God leads you to. You can do this in your church home, through a non-profit, or if God has called you to start your own ministry, it's best that you get to work.

Refuse to date. A woman of God should not keep company with a man who is just looking for personal entertainment. A woman of God should only agree to be courted by a man of God who is currently seeking God for His wife. It's important for you to be on guard during this process and seek God yourself as to who He wants you to give your heart to. Dating may place you in a spiritual bind that will hold you back from receiving your God ordained husband. When true courting takes place, both the man and the woman should be seeking God for confirmation as to whether He will approve of their union. Any man who is unwilling to go to your heavenly father to ask for you so He can be sure that you are his God ordained wife is a man you should discontinue your relationship with. Kingdom marriage is honorable before God, and it is a holy union that is ordained by Him. If a man won't seek God before the marriage, don't expect him to seek God when things get rough in the marriage. You are not your own to give away.

Set standards for the company you keep. You should know that you cannot entertain a man by simply watching a movie late at night alone. Such a man would not be thinking about the movie. He would be thinking about being affectionate with you. Being alone with a man is an opportunity for your passion to be awakened, and that passion is very hard to put to sleep once it has been aroused. The guilt and dirt you'll feel after the sin is simply not worth it.

Get an accountability partner. You do not have to go through this alone. You can have a sister in Christ keep you in check and accountable while you hold her accountable. If you find yourself in the middle of temptation, you need someone to help pull you about of the fire. Having an accountability partner is most successful when you have someone who is strongly connected to the Lord.

Clean out your contact list – This is an absolute must. More than likely, you have ties to people who do not have your best interest at heart. It is also likely that you have ties to counterfeits who are not the promise of God. They come to kill your self-esteem, steal your time and destroy your dreams of being happy, secure and loved.

Worship constantly and privately - Corporate worship at church is great, but it is not enough to sustain a relationship with Jesus Christ. It isn't enough to grab onto the power He has given you to beat sin with. There is something about the worship we do alone that brings about the blessings of the Lord. Worshiping alone places you far above others in your relationship with the Lord. Being in a private place, singing new songs to the Lord, entering into His presence with thanksgiving, worshiping on your knees and bowing your heart to show your honor to the King of kings opens the door to supernatural empowerment. The more intimate we are with the Lord, the more He will keep us empowered to reject the enemy. When you go into sincere worship with God, you step into His glory, and when you go into His glory, demonic residue falls off your soul and your appetite changes. This is why you'll find that some people may get upset with you for no reason and refer to you as high and mighty. You've gone higher than they have with the Lord, and the walk you walk is one that displays the mighty strength of the Spirit, and not the weakness of the flesh. The Bible states that we would be transformed by the renewing of our minds; the renewing process is in the spirit realm. We are able to grasp what God has for us in the spirit realm when we are in sincere worship.

Seek out deliverance in prayer for all things. Oftentimes, we know not what we should pray for, and when our prayer lives are barren, we will also find ourselves barren. The blessings of God are not being withheld from us. Sometimes, the problem is that we are somewhere that keeps us from receiving the blessings. We may not receive the blessing of good health because we might be bound to unhealthy foods. We might not receive the blessing of wealth because we are slothful or unorganized with our money. We might not receive the blessing of a God ordained husband because we have ungodly things in our lives that are unsuitable for a Godly relationship. We need to be Godly people if we want God to present us to men after His own heart. Men who happen to be trusting Him for their wives.

Watch what comes out of your mouth at all times! - Are you using profanity daily without realizing how near the Lord is to you? If so, your profane words could be covering your holy temple with darkness. Do you honestly think the Holy Spirit wants to be within an atmosphere where His royal priestess are cursing the same way the inhabitants of hell do? Absolutely not. If you cannot bridle your tongue, your religion is useless and of no effect.

Speak the promise of God over your life – Do you remember what I said earlier about the mouth gate? It is so important that you speak the blessings of the Lord into your atmosphere daily. Sometimes, the enemy encourages us to complain. Sometimes we are tempted to complain, but God has loved us so much that we have no right to complain before Him. Yes, God cares about our hearts, but an immature heart will not move Him. Sometimes, as women, we can get incredibly caught up in our emotions, especially when we're lonely. But God is more concerned about your heart being in the right position to receive all that He has for you than just giving you what you want just because you are acting like a toddler and throwing a tantrum. Find out what is being spoken by your spirit man first, and then, speak it out of your flesh. You will know what your spirit is saying because the spirit always seeks to please the Lord.

Ask God to keep you encouraged. – Sometimes we can make a choice to go in the wrong direction because we lack of faith and don't know what's in God's will for us. We've been in situations that have completely killed our dreams, and when this happened, it left us in a place of desperation. The

Bible states that we are to keep our courage at all costs. If we've lost courage, or lost hope in God's promise to us, we should ask Him for new courage. I once went through a very bad break up with a man who pumped my head up with lies about marriage and false dreams of having children. Once he committed to me, he began to intentionally crash our relationship, leaving me very humiliated and brokenhearted. I trusted God, but the way he did me made me feel as if I wasn't going to have any children anytime soon. I was discouraged and prayed for God to give me new hope. Because I prayed, God heard me, and He reassured me that my husband was on the way. He assured me that I would still have the children that were prophesied to me.

Know this... you cannot maintain your purity in your own strength. It is something that you must seriously partner with Christ about. Our minds are drawn to evil and God knows this. The Word says that He considered man and that the hidden counsels of his heart were continuously evil.

A formula of true repentance consists of prayer and pure worship. You have to believe that God will release the power of the Holy Spirit to keep you from the temptation of falling into sin.

Chapter 6

The Blessings in Store

The Blessing of Real Intimacy

When you've closed the doors on the things that are unlike God, there will be room for your best relationship ever. If you've ever experienced the honey moon stage of being married (finally) like I have, you'll know that one on the things you look forward to more than anything is alone time with your spouse. When you are with the one you love, you don't want anyone else around you and your mate. You think to yourself, "Finally, it's just us!" That's the feeling you can get out of an intimate relationship with the Lord when you forsake the way of the world. It is so important for Him to know you and for you to really know Him. You can't really know anyone you don't actually spend any time with.

The Blessing of His Favor

Even more important, know that God makes a distinction between professing believers who are holy and those who are unholy. When you are in obedience to God, you are in a cherished place with the Lord.

When you are obedient to God, you don't just get the scraps out of life that everyone else gets. Instead, God gives you the better portion. The Word says in Isaiah 1:19, "If ye be willing and obedient, ye shall eat the good of the land." You won't just eat the good off the land, but the "good" of the land. While others are in apartments, you will be building your dream home. Where others are shut out, you will have access. While others have rocky situations, your path will be made smooth. And while others have false intimate attachments to counterfeits and spouses who ignore God, you will have a man who is just right for your heart, because he is after God's own heart.

It makes no difference how far we feel we have gotten away from God and His plans, His love is a sure thing. His love perfects us, protects us, provides for us, comforts us, instructs us and guide us. His love for us cannot be corrupted in any way, form, or fashion.

The mistakes you may have made might have brought on some pretty dreadful consequences. But in those consequences are lessons that will guide you for the rest of your life if you would let them. Even though some lessons are incredibly dark and painful, they are full of the pearls of wisdom. After all, the Word states that all things work out for the good of those who love the Lord.

If you want God's best, you need to be God's best. No matter what you have been through, God can restore your life to fullness.

The Blessing of Wisdom

Consider something. God see's us all the time. He sees us every moment of the day. Even though we don't visually see Him, we can sometimes sense Him in the Spirit. If the way we demonstrate our love to Him is by obeying Him only when we can sense His presence, we really don't have a heart of faithfulness. Does God get angry with us? Absolutely. Does He judge us and place judgments on us? When we know better... yes! Does He chastise us? Absolutely. He wouldn't be a great Father if He didn't use His rod of correction to point us in the right direction. It absolutely breaks His heart when His children, whom He loves, stray from the path of salvation to do the works of the devil. To be able to repent is one of the most valuable gifts God has given us. It's more important than all the cars, clothes and money in the world. There have been so many people who'd lived lavish lifestyles that were full of sin, and those people are now dead and wishing they could hear the word "repent" one more time so they could change their eternal states.

The Blessing of Repentance

Once you've truly repented for a life of sin, a time of rest and restoration is usually necessary. No doubt, almost every woman desires to have a husband at some point in her life, but in order to obtain one, we must do things God's way. Just because you marry a man, does not mean that he is your husband. A husband covers and protects you from harm. A man who is fornicating with a woman is not protecting her from harm at all. He's simply polluting her with sin and exposing her to the dangers of hell's fire. While the world may see fornication or premarital sex as completely acceptable, this is not okay for God's women. God's women are called to holiness and righteousness. There are many women who say they want a man of God, but they behave like Jezebels around Godly men and encourage those men to sin. I'm not trying to place all of the blame on women because men can be Jezebels too, but we still have to do our parts in refusing to entice men and causing them to fall away from God. If we cause a man to fall away from God, usually one of two things will happen: That man will be with you only because you've allowed him to make you an idol. This will lead to him not having the relationship he needs with the Lord. He will grow closer to God and reject or look down upon you because you've been helping him to sin. Bottom line is that as vessels of the Lord, we are supposed to be agents of God and not the enemy. When we walk in the way of worldly women, we walk in rebellion. And rebellion is witchcraft.

The Heavy Price You Pay

One thing that real witches soon find out is that there is a heavy cost for the spiritual power they abuse to get what they want. When a woman of God is operating in witchcraft, there will always be a heavy price for her to pay for what she has done. Although God forgives you when you repent, the enemy will still come to collect the wages of your sin.

These things include:

Your name

Your marriage

Your time

Your health

Your possessions

Your children

Your home

And anything he can rightfully steal

The Bible clearly states that we cannot have two masters. For we will love one and hate the other. Jesus defines love as obedience to Him. God says that our obedience to Him means more to Him than our sacrifices. When we won't obey God, we are demonstrating hate, even if we profess to love Him. We say things with our mouth, but our hearts are far from Him.

But Jesus Died For My Sins!

Yes, Jesus did die for your sins because they are many. If it were not for Jesus, there wouldn't be enough sacrifices we could make to get right with God and enter heaven. But God cannot forgive you for sins that you are not truly repentant of. Repentant doesn't mean that you are sorry; repentant means that you are actively rejecting the error of your ways. As I've stated before, there is no way that we can remain holy in our own strength. I would know. It truly takes the power of the Almighty God to help us walk right, but we only find the strength to do so once we've completely and totally surrendered to Him.

The Blessing of Righteousness

Know this, there is no sin that will leave you when you are actively confessing that you love it. It is not a sin to love sex, but it is a sin to love fornication. **I love sex, but the idea of fornication repulses me for several reasons:**

Anytime I've had sex with a man, it meant I had just married that man in the realm of the spirit. Our souls are tied.

I know the pain all too well of having someone I've had sex with to leave my life. Fornication legally allows someone to take a piece of my soul and walk away with it.

When two people are together, they are "one flesh", meaning, they are now joined together in every way (spiritually and physically). They will share demons, fragments of the souls of their former lovers, DNA and personality traits.

When someone you've fornicated with cheats on you, it causes a deep tear in the soul tie you two share together, and the pain can be unbearable.

Fornication opens up satanic door-ways in your life that can cause you to lose the things you love.

Fornication leaves you with feelings of deep guilt and emptiness after it's over. You hope the person you've been intimate with loves and keeps you, but there are no guarantees.

God refers to sex as a man humbling us, meaning, he has lowered us beneath himself. For a man to humble you, and then, decide he won't be faithful to you, honor you as his wife, or stay with you is an incredibly painful situation to be in.

After you've been damaged by enough husbands and sex partners, you risk becoming unattractive in the spirit realm to a righteous man who is actually looking for a wife.

When you fully decide to do everything you can to walk after the righteousness of God, it's then you'll be a truly transformed woman because your mind has been renewed. When your mind has been renewed, your life will be renewed.

The Blessing of Knowing Better

God, being a good Father, rarely allows us to get away with anything. We must pay the price for every decision we make. Some decisions can bring us into complete and total ruin.

All around, the effects of fornication simply are not worth it. It's not worth it to your mind, body, or soul. Can these things happen in a marriage? Absolutely. But when you solely depend on God to lead your ordained mate to you and to keep your marriage happy, the likelihood of these things happening is minimal. Why? Your husband will love God first. He will love you with God's love because he can see you in the spirit. No other woman will be able to compare to you because nobody will be able to touch him the way God designed you to touch him.

For me personally, the decisions I made caused me several hardships and humiliations that I wouldn't wish on anybody. I'd worked hard, given my all, fasted, prayed and desperately wanted God to bring a type of healing to my life that I thought I would find in my husband. Being pregnant brought me the greatest joy I'd ever experienced in my entire life, but once I miscarried my first child, that miscarriage brought me the greatest grief I had ever experienced in my existence. The decisions I made brought me into the bondage of abuse, trauma, depression, suicidal thoughts, poverty and many other things. I'd lost my husband, my child, my home and my dreams for a stable family environment. I wept day and night for my dreams and desires of one day having a real family because I didn't have one growing up.

I had a lot of reasons for going down the path I chose for myself. God knows that if I were to go back in time, considering the family circumstances and social pressure I was under, there is no way I would've done things His way.

Why? I was really in darkness and unable to see any type of light except for the light I allowed myself to imagine. Nobody ever cared enough about me to tell me that God had a better way and I didn't have to lower my standards. I truly believed that if I just slept with the right man the right way, he would love me and keep me forever. Instead, I only found a man who lusted after me and wanted me as a personal possession. He didn't plan to honor me, and even after he said, "I do" he ferociously showed me that I was worthless to him. Because of what I know· now about Gods expectations of me, I will never make the mistake of walking in the fear of being alone. I will never place a man before Him ever again.

Holy Matrimony

God wants you to be married to a man of His choosing. He wants you to have children that are dedicated to Him for the building of the Kingdom, and He wants you to have the desires of your heart that are in line with His will for your life. He promises to be whatever it is that you need in your life. He promises to be both a Father and a Husband, meaning He will teach you and watch over you. You are His divine treasure here on this Earth. While we still have the grace of today, God helps us to clean up for tomorrow.

If you are thinking of getting married, it is very important that you have the right motives for marriage when asking God for your husband. If you are just looking for the help of someone to clear your debt, provide free housing to you, make you look better and be your personal sex toy, then you have a lot of growing in the Lord to do. Yes, every blessing our husbands give us is great, but it should not be the primary reason we desire to be married. The Word states in James 4:2-3 (NIV), "You desire but do not have, so you kill. You covet but you cannot get what you want, so you quarrel and fight. You do not have because you do not ask God. When you ask, you do not receive, because you ask with wrong motives, that you may spend what you get on your pleasures."

Just as God doesn't want to send you a man who is primarily looking to use you for sex, He doesn't want to send a righteous man to a woman who is in desperate need of marriage benefits.

What He desires for success in the Kingdom is to place together two holy people who are:

Focused on performing His will first.

Willing to forsake themselves so they can love each other.

Why? There is nothing more rewarding for mankind than doing the will of God, and the experience His love between a man and a woman. What a blessing for two people to interchangeably and constantly experience the power of God with one another. This is a reason the enemy works so hard to destroy, pollute and prevent marriages from being successful. A man and a woman who loves and obeys the Lord together are a force the kingdom of darkness cannot reckon with. Ecclesiastes 4:12 states, "And if one can overpower him who is alone, two can resist him. A cord of three strands is not quickly torn apart." This is the reason you need God in your marriage. Not only do you need Him in your marriage, you need His approval of your marriage.

I desire for you to be encouraged in your walk with the Lord. Although some days being obedient is tough, I know that the wages you pay for sin are even tougher. It's important, that you do not grow weary in your well doing. It's even more important that you do not despise the correction of the Lord. God pointing us in the right direction and redirecting us from the wrong paths is nothing short of a gift. It's true that God counts every single tear you have ever shed. He collects them in a special place and none of your tears go to waste when you are in Him. Living right and living in His light are the only ways for you to go if you are set on meeting Him in eternity. Do not let the enemy convince you that your only option is to go in his direction. Destroy your idols if you haven't. Turn away from the world. Get closer to Christ. Accept the call to serve Him first. Keep your purity, and walk in your blessing for today and for all of eternity. This is my love story. I've been wounded, but God called me to be better than man's expectations of me. I've been broken, but I've been restored because of God's forgiveness. And because of the sacrifice Jesus Christ made for me, all my sins have been atoned for. I've been blood-washed.

And yes, God actually did keep his Word to me. He brought my husband. I was the answer to his prayers. He loves me, protects me, cherishes me and we are living happily ever after.

About The Author

Alexa Jones is a wife, entrepreneur and prophetess residing in Tulsa, Oklahoma with her wonderful husband Roy Jones Jr and her 6 year old terrier Brownie. For the past 3 years, Alexa has been ministering, counseling and mentoring women on how to throw away sin, become closer to God and live a Godly life style through Bride of Christ International Ministries. Currently she host weekly Love, Sex & Marriage Webinars to help single women prepare for a marriage that still meets Gods standard of holiness. She also runs a Facebook group for single women called Kingdom Marriage that helps women prepare for their encounter with their God ordained mate. For the past 7 years she has been building various businesses including Roxi Virgin Hair Company and Brand Profit Studio where she develops high-end websites for busy business owners and non-profits.

You can follow Alexa's personal blog at www.iamalexajones.com.